MASCULINE SCENARIOS

MASCULINE SCENARIOS

edited by

Alcira Mariam Alizade

A Volume in the Psychoanalysis & Women Series
for the Committee on Women and Psychoanalysis
of the International Psychoanalytical Association

KARNAC

LONDON   NEW YORK

First published in 2003 by
H. Karnac (Books) Ltd.
6 Pembroke Buildings, London NW10 6RE

British Library Cataloguing in Publication Data

A C.I.P. for this book is available from the British Library

   ISBN 1 85575 962 4

10 9 8 7 6 5 4 3 2 1

Edited, designed, and produced by The Studio Publishing Services Ltd,
Exeter EX4 8JN

www.karnacbooks.com

CONTENTS

FOREWORD

COWAP, the Committee on Women and Psychoanalysis of the International Psychoanalytical Association, is both pleased and proud to present the third volume of this series of books, which provide a forum for discussion of issues involving sexuality, sexual identity, and gender constructs in a cross-cultural and international context.

The remit of the Committee is to investigate sexuality, interactions, and relationships between men and women. With this in mind, *Masculine Scenarios* aims to offer the reader a wide range of topics with their implications for the world of psychoanalysis. *Masculine Scenarios* discusses different issues involving object relations and their vicissitudes as regards the psychic world of men and male sexuality in general.

This book is intended to be open-minded and free-ranging in spirit. In putting forward their ideas, the authors hope that they will lead to fresh thinking and new hypotheses that stimulate the cross-cultural interplay of psychoanalysis and psychoanalytic ideas.

The contributors were selected on a basis that combined both chance and known professional skill, with the idea of theoretical pluralism uppermost in our minds, even though we realized that this would probably result in controversy.

The reader will find not only papers from different essentialist, constructivist, and culture-based standpoints, but will also note the existence of theoretical and clinical intersections where psycho-analysis borders on closely-related disciplines, such as philosophy, sociology, history, ethology, etc.

The biology that Nature bestows on each of us at birth, in its innocence and originality, provides the stage where human scenarios unfold. It is on this basis that the development of somatic, psychic, and socio-cultural integration is analyzed on various levels.

The body, that strange governor of our fate, gives expression to the voices inhabiting it. The inner discourse is that of our first significant others, with their trans-generational mandates and identificatory patterns. They speak to us through traumatic experiences and sexual feelings.

Historically, sexuality, as viewed by psychoanalysis, is wide-ranging and encompasses heterogeneous forms that involve subjectivity, scenarios recorded in the psychic flesh, and inevitable psycho-physical and cultural events.

In this series, classical areas of psychoanalysis are conjugated with postmodern questions and with new hypotheses to form a kind of heterogeneous, pluralistic spectrum defined to some extent by time and influenced by social factors that participate in the genesis and development of psychodynamics. The controversial concept of gender calls into question our established theories on sexuality and forces us to listen with an open mind to issues involving sexual identity and choice of sexual object.

This volume will enable the reader to venture on a stimulating journey into psychoanalytic terminology, cultural definitions, certainties, doubts, and hegemonies of all kinds. They oblige us to think and to think again about the complexity of sexuality in the light of psychoanalysis. Human identity, sexual identity, primary and secondary identification, object choice, narcissism—all of these lie on a continuum with homosexuality, transsexualism, transvest-ism, heterosexuality, and asexuality. Concepts on sexuality and gender are outlined anew in an interplay of theoretical and clinical networks, with the aim of increasing the efficiency of analytic *praxis* freed from prejudice and monolithic convention.

The hope of the Committee is that these papers will encourage future volumes with the aim of opening up further pathways into psychoanalytic exploration.

Alcira Mariam Alizade
Chairperson,
Committee on Women and Psychoanalysis of the
International Psychoanalytical Association.

CONTRIBUTORS

Alcira Mariam Alizade, M.D., is a psychiatrist and training analyst of the Argentine Psychoanalytic Association, Latin American co-chair of the IPA Committee on Women and Psychoanalysis (1998–2001) and current chair of the Committee on Women and Psycho-analysis of the International Psychoanalytical Association (COWAP). She is the author of *Feminine Sensuality* (Karnac Books, 1992); *Near Death: Clinical Psychoanalytical Studies* (1995); *Time for Women* (1996); *The Lone Woman* (1999); *Positivity in Psychoanalysis* (2002).

Jacqueline Amati Mehler trained in Adult and Child Psychiatry at Harvard University and is now a full-time practicing psychoanalyst. She is a training analyst and former President of the Italian Psychoanalytical Association (AIPsi) and founder of the Italian Journal *Psicoanalisi*. In 1988 she was a recipient of the Mary Sigourney Honorary Award. She is author of numerous clinical and theoretical publications, including a book, *The Babel of the Unconscious*, written with S. Argentieri and J. Canestri.

Colette Chiland is Emeritus Professor of Clinical Psychology in the René Descartes University of Paris, France (Paris V). She is currently a psychiatrist at the Alfred Binet Centre, Paris and a member of the Paris Psychoanalytical Society (S.P.P.).

Juan-Guillermo Figueroa-Perea, M.D., is a professor and researcher at the Centro de Estudios Demográficos y de Desarrollo Urbano of El Colegio de México. He has over twenty years experience working in areas related to reproductive behaviour and health, and has been coordinating seminars regarding "Ethics and reproductive health", "Women's reproductive rights" and "Sexuality, reproduction and health within the male perspective" in Mexico. He is also undertaking joint projects with NGOs on health and reproductive rights (of both women and men).

Martin Stephen Frommer, Ph.D., is a faculty member and supervisor in the psychoanalytic training program at the Institute for Contemporary Psychotherapy in New York City where he teaches in the areas of gender and sexuality. His articles have appeared in the journals *Psychoanalytic Dialogues, Studies in Gender and Sexuality, Journal of the American Psychoanalytic Association* and the *Journal of Gay and Lesbian Psychotherapy*, where he is a member of the Editorial Board. He maintains a private practice in Manhattan.

Águeda Giménez de Vainer, M.D., is a psychoanalyst. He is a full member, training analyst, and professor of the Argentine Psychoanalytic Association and a professor in the Department of Mental Health of the University of Buenos Aires.

Leticia Glocer Fiorini, M.D., is a full member and training analyst of the Argentine Psychoanalytic Association. She won the Association's Celes Cárcamo Prize (1993) for her paper: "The feminine position. A heterogeneous construction". She is author of *Lo Feminino y el Pensamiento Complejo* (2001) and co-author of *Escenarios Femeninos* (2000). Her papers on maternity and female sexuality were selected for presentation in the IPA Congresses in Santiago, Chile (1999) and Nice (2001) and published in the *Revista de Psicoanálisis*.

Jorge Kantor, is a clinical psychologist and a full member of the Peruvian Society of Psychoanalysis. He is professor of the Masters Programme at the Catholic University in Lima, Peru and coordinator of the residency department of the Center for Psycho-analytic Psychotherapy in Lima, Peru. He has published many papers including: "Reflexiones acerca de la intersubjetividad sexual, vincular y jerárquica entre hombres y mujeres", (2001) in IX Congreso sobre Subjetividad; and "Apuntes sobre la noción de paradoja en la obra de Donald Winnicott", (2001) in IX Congreso sobre Subjetividad.

Ruth F. Lax, Ph.D., A.B.P.P., is a fellow of the Institute of Psychoanalytic training and Research, a member of the New York Freudian Society, and a training and supervisory analyst. She is also a member, training and supervisory analyst of the International Psychoanalytical Association and a member of the American Psychoanalytic Association. She is author of *Becoming and Being a Woman*, Editor of *Essential Papers on Character Neurosis and Treatment*, senior editor of *Rapprochement: The Critical Subphase of Separation-Individuation* and of *Self and Object Constancy: Clinical and Theoretical Perspectives*. She has also published widely on masochism, character neurosis, issues in female psychosexual development, the menopause and psychic perspectives on aging, her areas of special interest. At present she is chair of the Committee on Psychoanalytic Aspects of Socially Sanctioned Violence Against Women.

Jaime M. Lutenberg is a training analyst of the Buenos Aires Psychoanalytical Association and works as a full-time psychoanalyst in private practice in Buenos Aires. He is a consultant teacher at the University and is a current member of the IPA Research Group on Borderline Patients, co-ordinated by André Green, which started in 2000. He has published over fifty psychoanalytical papers, in local and international journals. He is the author of *Psychoanalysis and Truth* (1998) and *The Void Ilusion* (2000).

Juan-David Nasio is a psychiatrist and a psychoanalyst.

John Munder Ross is a clinical professor and training analyst at the Columbia Center. He has published eight books, including *What Men Want* (1993) in which he describes two decades of his research on boys and men.

CHAPTER ONE

Sex and gender: the battle between body and soul

Colette Chiland

F reud stated that all human beings are bisexual in nature, though he did go on to say that each of us belongs a little more to one sex than to the other.

[Science] draws your attention to the fact that portions of the male apparatus also appear in women's bodies, though in an atrophied state, and *vice versa* in the alternative case. It regards their occurrence as indications of *bisexuality*, as though an individual is not a man or a woman but always both—merely a certain amount more the one than the other (1933a, p. 114).

If what Freud said is correct, a struggle between the two sexes is an ongoing feature of every human being's life. In some people, the dilemma is expressed in a very particular manner: the dichotomy—I would even go as far as to say the antagonism between factions—lies not between certain parts of the body nor between certain states of mind, but between mind and body as a whole. I am referring here, of course, to transsexuals.

In this chapter, I shall first discuss Freud's concept of bisexuality, then go on to explore how every human being has to process these issues in his or her own mind in order to construct a sense of identity. Finally, I shall develop some ideas concerning the transsexual's rejection of his or her genetic sex in an attempt to obtain "another" body, a "true" body that mirrors how the body is experienced in the mind.

Freud and bisexuality

Freud, as we know, wrote in German, and the German language does not make it easy to distinguish between "sex" and "gender", a distinction that first became prevalent in the 1950s. The word *Geschlecht* means both sex and gender. In a similar vein, German has only one adjective, *männlich*, for both "male" and "masculine", and *weiblich* for both "female" and "feminine". In French, as in English, it is up to the translator to choose—to interpret—whether to use one or the other pair of contrasting adjectives, male/female or masculine/feminine. This particular feature of the German language reinforced Freud's way of thinking, which anyway tended to give more weight to the biological aspect of sex rather than to its psychological and cultural dimensions.

It was with reference to embryology that Freud claimed that all human beings are bisexual. The Wolf and Müller ducts, present at the very beginning of intrauterine life, will later follow different paths, with the Wolf ducts developing in the male embryo and atrophying in the female one, while the Müller ducts grow in the female embryo and atrophy in the male. Freud insisted on the fact that the bud which later grows into a penis in the male has an undeveloped residue in the female—the clitoris. Thus, given that for Freud the clitoris is a male organ and not a truly female one, he could maintain that women are more clearly physically bisexual than men are. For this reason, he could make the somewhat surprising claim that, until puberty, "the little girl is a little man" (Freud, 1933a, p. 118), because of clitoral masturbation and of the fact that "for many years the vagina is virtually non-existent and possibly does not produce sensations until puberty" (Freud, 1931b, p. 228).

For Freud, then, if we superimpose the psychological categories of masculine and feminine on their biological counterparts of male and female, they make a perfect fit. Anything that involves the psychological level has to do with social convention and is subject to individual variation. Everything else is a function of the biological characteristics of the sex cells:

> You cannot give the concepts of "masculine" and "feminine" *any* new connotation. The distinction is not a psychological one; when you say "masculine", you usually mean "active", and when you say "feminine", you usually mean "passive". Now it is true that a relation of the kind exists. The male sex-cell is actively mobile and searches out the female one, and the latter, the ovum, is immobile and waits passively. This behaviour of the elementary sexual organisms is indeed a model for the conduct of sexual individuals during intercourse. The male pursues the female for the purpose of sexual union, seizes hold of her and penetrates into her. [Freud, 1933a, p. 114]

Freud uses the term bisexuality, however, in another sense, relating to homo- and heterosexual tendencies—identification with the father and the mother in their erotic dimension, particularly in the complete version (positive and negative) of the Oedipus complex.

It would appear, therefore, that in both sexes the relative strength of the masculine and feminine sexual dispositions is what determines whether the outcome of the Oedipus situation is an identification with the father or with the mother. This is one of the ways in which bisexuality takes a hand in the subsequent vicissitudes of the Oedipus complex [...] Closer study usually discloses the more complete Oedipus complex, which is twofold, positive and negative, and is due to the bisexuality originally present in children: that is to say, a boy has not merely an ambivalent attitude towards his father and an affectionate object-choice towards his mother, but at the same time he also behaves like a girl and displays an affectionate feminine attitude to his father and a corresponding jealousy and hostility towards his mother (Freud, 1923b, p. 33).

Freud did not deal with the particular case of those whom we nowadays call intersexed. In his view, we all possess bisexual components, and it is up to each of us to enable our male and female aspects to coexist within the self. That said, we cannot avoid coming up against the "underlying bedrock" of our biological nature—penis envy in women and, in men, the masculine protest, linked to castration anxiety, and repudiation of femininity (Freud, 1937, p. 252).

The two elements of the opposing male/female couple are not in a symmetrical relationship. There is undoubtedly some extra value attributed to the male/masculine/phallic dimension, whilst the female/feminine/female genital sphere is quite clearly treated as having less value. Freud emphasized the envy women feel with respect to men, but said very little about the envy men may experience with respect to women's capacity for motherhood.

The construction of gender identity

The concept of identity played no part in Freud's thinking. Even though all human beings may be bisexual, gender identity in the individual is based on the predominance of one of these dimensions over the other. There is a narcissistic continuity that determines how the individual experiences his or her envy and fear of the opposite sex. The fact that a girl experiences penis envy does not imply that she wants to be a boy; she wants to go on being herself, while at the same time enjoying all the advantages she attributes to boys: thanks to their possession of a penis, they can urinate standing up and play at who can pee the farthest; they can manipulate their genitals and check that masturbation has not damaged them; parents seem to prefer boys (this is undoubtedly the case in some societies, where girl babies may even be put to death); and they enjoy the kind of freedom and social privileges that are denied girls (this has changed in western societies, but only fairly recently).

How do boys and girls reach the conclusion that they are indeed boys or girls? The experience of one's own body is distinctive. In spite of all the embryonic residues, a baby does not experience his or her body as bisexual in nature, but as something in itself absolute. The baby boy does not realize that his experience is not identical to that of a baby girl, and *vice versa*. Before he is able to make a connection between this experience and his biological gender, he will have been looked at, handled, encouraged or discouraged in a thousand ways to go on (or to stop) doing such-and-such; and the same is true of the baby girl. Babies are shaped by their parents and bombarded with conscious and unconscious messages that they then have to interpret. Some children are more resilient and unwilling to submit, others are more easily influenced. Parents unwittingly give both positive and negative reinforcement to behaviour patterns they consider to be masculine- or feminine-oriented in their children. It is only later that the infant becomes able to establish a connection between his or her experience and the label "boy" or "girl". The distinction comes from outside the self. The discovery that there are two sexes is a traumatic one. The fact that boys and girls have different genitalia is acknowledged at some point between eighteen-months and two-years of age (Roiphe & Galenson, 1981). Though children know that this is an important difference, for a long time to come they will remain unable to mention it if they are questioned about the differences between boys and girls.

Children have to make the continuity of their experience both meaningful and significant. A feeling of continuity will be possible only if the environment is sufficiently coherent, and it is only if the child is given some feeling of personal value that the ability to love and appreciate him- or herself can arise.

Even though boys and girls are brought up together in kindergarten or nursery school from age two or three onwards, for impromptu games in the playground a spontaneous segregation between the two sexes is quickly established (Maccoby, 1988, 1990). It would appear that once children have made the traumatic discovery that there are two sexes, they stay with their same-sex peer group in order to obtain reassurance and increase their self-esteem while denigrating the opposite sex; Maccoby emphasizes, in particular, the fact that both sexes do not use the same modes of communication. The tendency to denigrate the opposite sex runs from elementary school all the way through to adolescence, at which point sexual attraction and mutual seduction begin to play a role (Baudelot & Establet, 1992).

With the exception of intersexed individuals, in whom the different components of sexuality are at odds with each other—with the resultant dilemma either of having to make a decision as to the gender of the individual at birth (given the fact of genital ambiguity) or of discovering at puberty that development is not following the expected path—no difficulty as regards integrating biological bisexuality exists. It is *psychological* bisexuality that creates the conflict, the kind of bisexuality that Freud failed to address. It is not simply a matter of sexual orientation via identification with the parental figures, but of identification with the psychological masculine and feminine features of each of the parents and with what society as a whole determines to be masculine and feminine.

The fact, for example, that girls want to follow the same academic courses as boys and take up the same careers cannot, as has been done in the past, be attributed simply to penis envy. A woman can experience herself as female, be happy to be a woman, be heterosexual—and still fight for equal rights. To put it another way, accepting the difference between the sexes, in all of its ramifications, does not preclude the struggle for equal rights.

Nevertheless, a woman often experiences feelings of guilt relating specifically to being, in the fullest sense, a woman and a mother, while at the same time gaining access to the highest levels of skill and competence in her chosen career—possessing not only feminine characteristics, but also those that society over the centuries has defined as distinctively phallic.

Sex and the battle between body and soul

Is it legitimate to think of a sex of the soul, or a sex of the mind? Those who use one or the other of these terms to refer to themselves are thereby indicating that their whole existence—soul and mind— is tied to the contradiction between the identity they feel themselves to possess and their anatomical sex. Their experience is that of a woman trapped inside a man's body, or of a man similarly trapped inside a woman's body. They sometimes go as far as to say that "this" body is not in fact their own and that their "true" body ought to be "restored" to them.

From time immemorial, there have been men and women who reject the sex that nature has attributed to them, without this having anything to do with the well-known biological condition called intersex. Some have managed to live as members of the "opposite" sex.

Historically, some civilizations have made allowance for—or at least tolerated—the fact that certain individuals may belong to a third sex or gender, and some contemporary societies still do (Herdt, 1994; Chiland, 1997). Examples of this are the North American Indian berdache, the Inuits, the Hijras, etc.

Transsexualism, as a modern phenomenon, is characterized by the fact that medical practitioners can offer to reassign an individual's sex by means of hormone treatment and surgery; this has been made possible by our increasing knowledge of hormones and by the development of cosmetic surgery (Hausman, 1995).

The aetiology of transsexualism, however, is still a mystery. Two hypotheses are usually put forward; one is purely biogenetic, the other, while accepting the potential importance of as yet undiscovered biological factors, lays more emphasis on interrelationships. The element common to both hypotheses is the idea that, very early on in life, something happened that caused the individual to identify his or her body as male or female in nature, yet at the same time to refuse to accept it as his or her own, i.e. as in keeping with the mind's experience of gender and with the self's subjective identity. Such individuals find themselves in an extremely distressing situation, and communication with other people is undoubtedly difficult.

Communication with medical practitioners is difficult. Transsexuals do not think of themselves as suffering from some mental disorder or other. They consult a doctor because they want reparative treatment, one that will restore their true body, the body that corresponds to their soul and mind. Though the physician may be able to change the outward appearance of the patient's body to a more or less credible extent, there is no way medicine can change the "inner" body or the patient's past experience of it.

Some transsexuals—but they are few and far between—seem immediately to grasp this situation and declare themselves satisfied to "live as a woman" (in the case of male-to-female transsexualism) or "as a man" (in the case of female-to-male transsexualism). Others make the slow and painful discovery that anatomical change is limited in scope; they may not regret having had surgery, but they are, nevertheless, to some extent dissatisfied and find themselves still having to cope with many difficult issues.

The media proclaim: "Nowadays, a man can be changed into a woman, and a woman into a man!" On their television screens, they present people who are histrionic—and far removed from those who have no wish to publicize their condition.

Militants advocate the surgical solution and argue for it to be more widely available. But in claiming "I'm a woman (or a man), and I've always been a woman (a man)", all they are really doing is trying to eliminate the complex nature of the problem they face.

Transsexuals are sometimes said to belong to both sexes, in the sense that they embody one sex while in their mind they feel they belong to the opposite sex. But, in fact, they are highly intolerant of psychic bisexuality: they try above all to get rid of anything that might remind them of the sex they loathe and to forget everything that has to do with their past life as members of the sex they reject.

As regards the libidinal bisexuality of their sexual orientation, some transsexuals have no sex life at all; those who have sexual relations with partners of the same biological sex as theirs see these relations as heterosexual—because it is as members of the *opposite* sex that they love people who belong to the same biological sex as they do. There are very few transsexuals who claim to be homosexual—for example, a man changed into a woman who calls h/self "lesbian" and has sexual relations exclusively with women.

In an attempt to understand the enigma of transsexualism, a fair amount of research has been undertaken, including post-mortem anatomo–pathological examination of the brain in male-to-female transsexuals (Zhou *et al.*, 1995) and the study of the consequences of *in utero* hormone impregnation in animals (Goy *et al.*, 1988). These studies would appear to indicate that transsexuals are in fact intersexed individuals who have not been identified as such.

The findings of these studies are, as yet, difficult to interpret. Zhou *et al.*'s research is based on the acknowledged importance in animals of the central subdivision of the bed nucleus of the stria terminalis—this is particularly true of rodents, where it is known to control sexual posturing. Its role in human beings, however, is much less clear, and the authors agree that there is no accepted animal model for gender identity. Furthermore, only six brains were available for examination over an eleven-year period; it proved impossible to show that the volume of the central subdivision of the bed nucleus of the stria terminalis—smaller in these transsexuals than that found in men, comparable to or smaller than that found in women—had not changed since birth, and was a cause rather than a consequence of the transsexual lifestyle and treatment programmes.

Zhou *et al.* argue that the variation in volume of this tiny brain area is compatible with potential hormone influence *in utero* such as that discovered by Goy *et al.* in female rhesus macaques.

Here again, having recourse to animal models in order to study gender identity is not without problems, even though monkeys have more in common with human beings than have rats. Observed behaviour is the only source of data: though females androgenized early or late in life do present certain behaviour patterns typical of males, none can be said to behave entirely as a male would. There are cases where androgenization has occurred *in utero* (congenital adrenal hyperplasia) in human beings; in girls, there is some morphological alteration to their external genitalia, they tend to be more tomboyish in behaviour, and homosexuality is slightly more prevalent, but their basic self-identity is quite clearly feminine.

When children who reject their assigned gender without there being any manifest intersex problem are seen in consultation, and if their parents are willing to co-operate in the treatment, the part played by parent–child interactions can be observed *in vivo*. Psychotherapy is possible as long as each of the parents is helped, as well as the child. The parents themselves make progress and acquire some insight into the impact on their child's refusal to accept his or her anatomical gender of what they themselves felt, said or did in the past; this is essential if the changes experienced by the child in the therapy are to last. Such clinical experiences lend weight to the hypothesis stating that interactions with the environment play a significant role in the development of transsexualism.

Conclusion

Is it still true to say, as Freud argued, that, biologically speaking, all human beings are bisexual, with the male element taking precedence over the female?

In more recent times, some authors have argued that it is in fact the *female* element that is pre-eminent. Mary-Jane Sherfey (1966), for example, states that for the first six weeks the human embryo is female because it develops along female lines—in spite of its X–Y chromosomic formula—in the absence of any active intervention by the antimüllerian factor and by male hormones. Other writers speak rather more accurately of the embryo being undifferentiated. In any case, the crucial epistemological error here lies in the fact that the psychological component is thought of as deriving directly from the biological, thereby ignoring the fact that there exists a hiatus between biology and psychology and that this hiatus requires the intervention both of the mind and of cultural factors. It is for this reason that we cannot simply superimpose the contrasting pairs male/female and masculine/feminine.

It is still possible to say that some elements are bisexual in nature, because both types of sex hormone are present in both men and women, though in considerably different quantities. However, on the psychological level, it is identification with the father and mother, as well as with gender-oriented cultural values, that creates a significant degree of bisexuality, which is in itself a source of conflict.

The extreme case of transsexualism is not a conflict *stricto sensu* between two aspects of the mind—which is why transsexuals do not, in general, seek psychoanalytic help; there is a dichotomy between anatomical and psychological sex leading to a complete rejection of one of the two. In order to convince themselves of the authenticity of their experience, transsexuals have to force out of their mind anything that could possibly remind them of their anatomical sex. Hence, a particular characteristic shared by almost all transsexuals, however different they may be as individuals, is that they claim to have no memory of their childhood, and sometimes go as far as to say—revealingly—that they do not *want* to remember their childhood. This is not simply repression plus the return of the repressed, nor is it mere reluctance; it is a deliberate wish *not* to remember, with the sometimes successful aim of bringing about a split that contributes to upholding their denial of the fact that one cannot change one's body.

Reintegration of these elements expelled from the mind sometimes occurs when, after surgery, such patients come to analysis because of the difficulties they then encounter in living their new identity to the full (Quinodoz, 1998).

At first sight, to argue that psychological and cultural factors play a major role in the constitution of gender identity would seem to run counter to Freud's hypothesis of the pre-eminence of biological factors. However, we find ourselves in agreement with him when he claims that all we can ever know about the unconscious is what is organized via verbal representations. A man or a woman is not simply a male or a female, nor someone who plays a masculine or feminine role to perfection, as would an impersonator; a man or a woman is a male or a female who conforms at least in part to current social stereotypes. The intersexed and the transsexuals are in a distressing and almost untenable situation.

CHAPTER TWO

Men and their bedrock: "repudiation of femininity"[1]

Alcira Mariam Alizade

Introduction

This paper discusses the repudiation of femininity as evidenced in the clinical material of a male patient.

Freud often emphasized the problem that human beings, particularly men, have with femininity. He wrote:

> It is to be suspected that the essentially repressed element is always what is feminine. This is confirmed by the fact that women as well as men admit more easily to experiences with women than with men. What men essentially repress is the paederastic element. [1897, Draft M, p. 251]

He returned to the subject in the last years of his life in "Analysis Terminable and Interminable" (1937) where, in the final chapter, he introduced the concept of "bedrock". Bedrock represents the outer limit of analysis. It is a representational–affective complex that psychoanalytic work cannot fail to come up against, and characterizes the point at which the analytic approach can no longer operate.

According to Freud, both men and women patients experience these limitations. In women, the bedrock is represented by penis envy, while in men it is "repudiation of femininity" (*Ablehnung der Weiblichkeit* in German, Freud, 1937, Chap. 8). *Ablehnung* has variously been translated into Spanish as "disauthorization" (*Amorrortu*), "rejection" (*Santiago Rueda*) or "repudiation" (*Biblioteca Nueva*). I would like to add the milder connotation in the original German of "putting aside" or "refusal of a request".[2] When men are offered the possibility of taking on board the feminine position, they say "I pass". The femininity they refuse constantly inhabits them and, through repetition, returns time and again in search of a way out via integration.

The man's conflict with femininity oscillates between fascination and vehement rejection. To my way of thinking, the scope for rejection of femininity is very wide. Freud claimed that it indicated the man's "struggle against his passive or feminine attitude to another male" (1937, p. 250), adding: it "can be nothing else than a biological fact, a part of the great riddle of sex" (*ibid.*, p. 252).

In many cases, the femininity that men reject goes beyond the negative Oedipus complex. It encompasses a massive degree of repudiation (foreclosure) and denigration that, whether conscious or unconscious, is always there, and aimed at any reference to attributes of the feminine sphere. This dimension is associated with passivity and homosexual tendencies in men (in other words, their feminization).

Penis envy and the rejection of femininity have their roots in the difference between the sexes. Both sexes reject femininity and take refuge in valuing what is phallic. The bedrock is set up as a powerful defence. Women find it difficult to renounce the ardent desire to obtain a phallus–penis, while men set great store by rejecting femininity and upholding a phallic standpoint.

In the light of these considerations, the phallus, embodied in the masculine position, soon establishes itself as the highest wish of every individual, man or woman.

Femininity and the feminine and masculine positions

Epithets, such as enigmatic, mysterious, and servile, have been attributed to women, those inhabitants of the "dark continent" (Freud, 1926b). Because, traditionally, the path followed by female erotogenicity was considered to be incomprehensible, scientific discourse has tended to categorize it as paradoxical and difficult.

The physical weakness of women and their role as bearer of life and death (through the adventure of motherhood) contributed to placing the word "female" in the same category as vulnerable, inferior, denigrated, and unknown.

The vicissitudes of the female body generate fantasies of death and mystery. The direct link with blood—in menstruation, defloration, and childbirth—also contributes to create ideas of submission to violence and of wounded, injured flesh. Freud spoke of the emergence of female masochism (1924), also found in men, and showed how it is focused on three physical events: "being castrated, or copulated with, or giving birth to a baby" (Freud, 1924b, p. 162). These female occurrences are supposedly connected with pain and feeling defenceless and constitute an imaginary biology, the aim of which is to enact scenes of bodily suffering.

The feminine sphere lends itself to personifying the great riddle of creation, coinciding with the first childhood question that Freud (1908a) highlighted: "Where do children come from?" Freud claimed that the idea of the universal penis blocks access to the answer to this question. He showed clearly how the infant attributes a penis to the woman at exactly the point where he or she intuits the presence of an internal container for producing babies. The orifice, the vaginal tunnel, the *via regia* that leads to the productive interior of women, becomes representable, but in an unbearable manner. Once again, our anatomy is our destiny; in this case, the female body generates anxiety-producing fantasies, with ancestral fears being projected onto it. The feminine dimension ushers in the idea of castration and encompasses the domain of concrete reality. In order to avoid this mental upheaval, women must also be thought to have a penis. The idea that "everyone has a penis" is established with all the conviction of certainty because of the specific need to alleviate mental distress in both sexes.

The feminine sphere is almost impossible to represent and unbearable, evoking castration on the one hand and, on the other, emptiness, as it borders on concrete reality and the uncanny. To a certain extent, the lack of being that constitutes the human condition is made flesh (Alizade, 1991, 1992a).

To speak of femininity is to speak of life and death. The perishable nature of the body is clear in passivity, in female surrender, in the acceptance of weakness and finitude. Women's aesthetic mask disguises the horror that we all feel when faced with a decidedly non-aesthetic, decomposing body: a corpse.

Femininity also has to do with giving and generosity. Women give their bodies, their efforts—and sometimes their life—in child-birth, in breast-feeding, in bringing up children, in that invisible work that is often devalued in the eyes of the phallic-centred culture that can see only visible power and the gloss of possessing narcissistic ornaments (money, consumer goods, prestige, glory).

But it is not only the feminine dimension that women embody. In the image of the phallic mother, they are endowed with inordinate completeness and extreme idealization. The woman then becomes *everything*. The phallic mother removes women from the purely feminine sphere and clothes them in a fantasy of exorbitant power, anchored in the omnipotence of bisexuality.

Unadorned femininity is experienced as a narcissistic wound, because it constitutes a space in which people have to come to terms with their finitude and mysterious being in the world. "The most touchy point in the narcissistic system, the immortality of the ego" (Freud, 1914, p. 91) is shaken.

Masculinity often functions on the phallic level, the signifier of something lacking (Lacan, 1958) that refers to power and narcissistic symbols. This lack, however, is obstructed by what is experienced as visible and prominent (the erect penis)—virility and strength, penetration, certainty.

The phallus attempts to conceal deficiencies. It moves over the surface of the senses, impressing them with a soothing character, because of the feeling of potency it involves. Necessary throughout the vicissitudes of life, it must also come to terms with the other side of existence where another, non-phallic order reigns: the female one.

Feminine and masculine positions interact in the psyche. Their integration is a basic condition for easing the battle between the sexes, thereby making life itself more pleasurable. Anchored in biology, the masculine sphere involves strength, activity, posses-sion, acquiring, and winning. The woman's domain is that of submission, servility, suffering, inferiority, life, death, vulnerability, the enigmatic, and the invisible (Alizade, 1992c). It comes, therefore, as no surprise that the "bedrock" at stake in both sexes has to do with the refusal to accept femininity.

Presentation of Ivan

Ivan consulted me because he felt that "shit" had invaded his life. He is a pleasant young man who, nonetheless, feels extremely unhappy. He compulsively abandons himself to drinking, gambling, work, and women. States of intense depression were triggered by the collapse of his ideals: in one case, when his aloof but idealized father attempted suicide after losing a considerable sum of money, in another, when he lost his job without any explanation. As Ivan himself put it, the great family cartel suddenly fell apart.

He is the elder of two children. When he was a baby, he was very close to his mother. A first narcissistic wound occurred when his sister was born (Ivan was three-years-old at the time), arousing intense jealousy in him. He adores his mother and tells her everything that happens to him; he feels possessed by and dependent on her. He remembers that when he was about five, he played at being a woman, putting on his mother's under-slip.

Based on this fantasy, the different threads of his Oedipus complex were woven in both positive and negative directions.

To Ivan, women always seemed to possess many privileges: his mother, the focus of the household, exercised complete authority and was strictly obeyed (imago of the phallic mother), while his younger sister usurped the parents' love.

Ivan is someone with a large quantity of libido (Freud, 1908b), who very early in life formed a hysteric-type envelope of excitation (A. Anzieu, 1987). He would take his afternoon naps with his paternal grandmother, and this was a stimulus for his first erection when he snuggled up to her buttocks in the double bed. He remembers these episodes with a mixture of guilt and pleasure.

When he reached puberty, his father remained aloof; Ivan laments this absence of "body contact" with his father, which might have allowed the adolescent to identify with him and accept his masculinity. His "man to man" sex games included playfully pressing his penis against the buttocks of a schoolmate or watching as a neighbourhood homosexual caressed a friend. He constantly sought to affirm his place as a "smart guy" who knew all the ins and outs and could teach other men the secrets of erotic life.

His cousins introduced him to having sex with prostitutes when he was thirteen. He became an expert in brothel culture and boasts about it. Now married, his activity with prostitutes has a compulsive quality that calms him down whenever he feels anxious. He knows several "madams" who phone him to recommend new girls who might suit his tastes.

The idea that he can have permanent access to a woman's body is vital to him.

He has had only one girlfriend, now his wife, whom he admires and loves. They have two children.

His language constantly focuses on references to the body. He is like a perverse polymorphous child, excitable and prone to tantrums, with no containing skin-ego (D. Anzieu, 1985).

Ivan's difficulty in symbolizing, and his many bodily codes, lead me to think in terms of a pre-neurotic pathology in someone who is searching for symbols that would enable him to be rid of the envelope of excitation and to reach a higher level of mentalization.

Ivan and femininity.
The "prostitute complex" and the "Oedipus complex"

Ivan used his body to illustrate the vicissitudes of the visible aspects of his Oedipus complex.

The materiality of bodies is fundamental to psychic structuring. Touching and not touching generate psychic movements, while representations and affects interact with the predominant role played by sensuality, feelings, and perception. The Oedipus complex is always present in experiences of touching and not touching, caressing and rejecting, disgust and sensual attraction, indifference to contact and heightening of sensory excitement.

Without this "body to body" interaction, psychic structuring is impossible. The other person's body can represent a positive or negative pole in the management of early anxieties. A crucial point is the exchange of identifications with the other person's body; scenarios are played out in which the one individual in fact represents the second character, while the other's body creates or recreates the potential for relationships. Through his or her similarity, the other person becomes a mirror reflecting different fantasies, and identificatory movements project scenes and introduce diverse latent roles that are subsumed in the manifest aspect of the relationship.

"Body to body" communication with meaningful others (father–mother–siblings, etc.) generates a mind–body space, an interactive zone in which the erogenous–affective body (Alizade, 1992c) has an important participatory role to play in laying the seeds of identification.

Freud (1910–1912) described one kind of splitting typical of men's erotic life: the idealization of the mother–woman goes hand in hand with the denigration and reparation ("saving") of the prostitute–lover–woman. The sensual and tender currents follow different paths. Behind the figure of the prostitute, via repressed incestuous fantasies, the shadow of the mother can be discerned. The maternal complex and the prostitute complex are interrelated.

The man who is afraid of his own femininity avoids any possibility of contagion by that of his wife. With the prostitute this avoidance is facilitated, because for the most part she plays by masculine rules. She claims to "know" the art of obtaining pleasure, entices her clients with superficial lures, one of which in fact is the financial aspect as applied to sexual commerce, as well as negotiation and the use of her body as an object of exchange in the service of paid work. She toils while giving her client pleasure.

Ivan has a deficit in symbolization. Caught in the vicissitudes of the oedipal drama, he uses the erogenous body of paid women to enact what he has failed to integrate intrapsychically. He seeks a way, via the flesh/body of others, of working through his anxiety in an attempt to obtain relief. His identificatory insufficiency is expressed by unconscious compulsive demands on the "other body", which acquires fundamental importance as a support for his psychic equilibrium.

The multiplicity of his identifications is evident in the space of the "prostitute complex". By this I am referring to a set of "... congeries of ideas and its associated affect" (Freud, 1910c, p. 234). I will try to describe its component aspects.

Prostitutes function in various ways in Ivan's life: (1) they give him pleasure; (2) they allow him to act out scenarios that structure his identificatory interplay; and (3) they provide narcissistic reassurance.

His description of prostitutes stems from two basic points of view:

(a) those who are maternal–feminine—good, simple, affectionate women, friends, and often mothers. They calm his anxiety and stimulate his narcissism by praising his masculine attributes and making him feel that with him "it's different", meaning that they give him preferential treatment. He is a kind of "favourite child" of these prostitute mothers. He remembers them with affection, recalling their names and virtues.

(b) those who are phallic–masculine—women who, he claims, have high social status and sell themselves only for pleasure, women who are beautiful and triumphant, or again women who coldly negotiate with their bodies.

When he is in a brothel, Ivan puts his phallicism into action, thereby alleviating his castration fantasies. His compelling need to confirm his manliness recalls what Freud had to say (1937, p. 251): "... the passive attitude, since it presupposes an acceptance of castration, is energetically repressed, and often its presence is only indicated by excessive overcompensations".

Ivan's excessive overcompensation testifies to the efforts he has to make in order to keep his feminine components repressed.

They are evidenced in his favourite brothel scenario: a woman sucks his penis and swallows his semen. Besides the pleasure obtained with the erogenous body, there is a fantasy of taking the mother's place and nourishing a child with his penis–breast. This fantasy rapidly became conscious in the course of his analysis. Another kind of couple appears in the scenario in which Ivan asks to be penetrated anally by the woman's tongue. This scene refers to the negative Oedipus complex: penetration by the penis–tongue.

In the reassuring setting of his phallicism (the brothel) he can give free rein to his fantasy world and act out his bisexual demands with his erogenous body.

Man–mother–woman, mother–child, man–father, is the series of images that emerge through the narration of his adventures in the brothel, and are worked on in the analysis. A whole range of identificatory illusions unfolds between Ivan and the prostitutes. In the interaction between fantasy and reality, imaginary scenarios are set up in which the vicissitudes of oedipal and pre-oedipal fantasies are played out.

Ivan refuses his wife's femininity and, in their erotic intimacy, he treats her roughly "as if she too were a whore". He asks her with "virility" to suck his penis, uses vulgar language "that she doesn't like" and avoids the emergence of affects that might evoke an attitude of feminine weakness.

He needs women to adopt either a phallic or a denigrated-feminine position. What must not occur is anything evocative of femininity, whether in the acceptance of the enigma, the unknown, the mysterious, the sexual ecstasy, or in *the glow of femininity in the affirmation of incompleteness* (Alizade, 1992c).

Ivan often talks about his fear of death, the "axe" as he calls it, a clear reference to castration. Human misery and failings drive him to despair. His obsessionality drives him to want to construct an orderly, unchanging, safe world.

Ivan's weakness in resolving his Oedipus complex could be described as follows: alternating between the positive and negative aspects of the Oedipus complex, he attempts to break free of his homosexual fantasies and to reaffirm his masculine vigour via a somewhat peculiar erotic life. When he relates to a woman sexually, he has to do away with repressed elements, which nonetheless return. Though he tries to escape from the "feminine" woman, he finds her again on his own body. He is afraid that he might perceive himself as vulnerable and mortal if he were to take on board his own feminine aspects. He would like once and for all to be rid of the feminine sphere. Phallic components alone should reign, because the sight of anything to do with the feminine sphere or other signifiers of his mother's body (Van Buren, 1992) give rise to intense anxiety.

Frequent allusions to "shit" in his sessions refer to anything dirty, impure, incomplete, and imperfect that he meets in everyday life.

In order to resolve his Oedipus complex, Ivan will have to integrate the symbolic castration he is constantly attempting to avoid by triumphing over the castration fantasy, via his multiple sexual relations.

The denigration of femininity exacerbates his phallicism. Women are worthless, a residue, waste matter, an object to use then throw away. Behind the emptiness that he tries to play down lurks "nothingness" (Alizade, 1992b), the invisible power of another order evocative of the impossible, the multiple unknowns of existence and the ephemeral nature of individuality, perhaps even of the entire human species. This is the "axe" Ivan mentions so frequently, meaning something that will put an end to pretending—when human beings face the blade of that particular axe, they catch a glimpse of a far-off light, a glimmer, a candle that illuminates the road to wisdom.

The analysis

Every analysis involves a "body to body" interaction between analyst and patient in the space of the sessions and in the setting of the transference. This "hand to hand" struggle develops a sensorial network of fantasies. In respecting the rule of abstinence, the body-words touch and explore the analysand's psycho-corporeity. Given that "the ego is above all a bodily ego" (Freud, 1923b), if we accept that the skin ego (D. Anzieu, 1985) is a precursor of this bodily ego, behind the ostensible ignoring of bodies that the analytic setting imposes, a fundamental sort of encounter takes place between two beings—in all of their multifarious aspects—who have embarked on the work of unveiling the unconscious. A common skin is created between them, a containing psychic envelope, inside which analysis of the contents takes place.

In the main, Ivan's language was made up of words referring directly to the body. His metaphors were physical, his symbolism weak. The envelope that his excitation shaped, like a skin-ego sieve, filtered out the disorganization that his instinctual drives threatened. Drive representations constructed oral, anal, and phallic fantasies out of diverse objects that were substitutes for primary incestuous relationships.

Ivan threw, so to speak, a mantle of excitation over the analyst, generating an atmosphere in the sessions that was impregnated by the erogenous body and its secretions. He was uncomfortable during the hot summer weather, and he wondered how I could listen quietly to his intimate erogenous secrets without myself concurring in his invitation to excess (supporting the paternal function).

Here are some extracts from different sessions that illustrate the points I have been making:

"Mamma had balls, she gave dad shit all the time, he never got hot and bothered about my grades, I always shifted for myself."

"I never even farted without telling my old lady about it."

"I realize I've got a suit of armour that keeps me from loving my wife. As if she were a whore and inside I'm dying to give her everything, though something else keeps me from doing it."

"They always had to go and put their cock up my ass."

"I've got a whorehouse of ideas."

"Sometimes I see myself as a whore, a hooker. Everybody says I look girlish."

"Sometimes I get up and I'm cocky."

"I'm going to be a prostitute and that's it."

"I'm impulsive and hot-tempered ... like a hooker." "I'm waiting for the axe ... sometimes when I wake up I'm thinking about dying."

"I think you're a weirdo. How can you not get really hot? You're a weirdo."

Gradually, through the analysis of this highly ostentatious material, the envelope of excitation began to dissolve and Ivan began to incorporate the paternal function and to organize his psyche. He was able to unify the sensual and tender currents, thus freeing himself of the harmful effects of the maternal complex. Femininity, which confronted him with weakness and death (the famous "axe"), was partially incorporated into working through the castration complex.

The following is an extract from one session:

Ivan: I stayed at home sucking on a beer alone, I went haywire, anxiety, I felt ill again, I looked at my body expecting illness, expecting the axe ... maybe if it weren't for my family I might shoot myself ... again, the doubts if I get hysterical, I say to myself, what the shit is this all about, I was doing so fine [brief silence]. I dreamed about a high-class little blonde whore who was sucking my cock. I grabbed her head and said, "Suck, suck, suck ..."

When my wife menstruates, I don't like it ... no, no ... I fell into the shit, motherfucker ... I never grew up, never grew up ... I'm not aware I'm a father ... that's crummy ... I never changed my daughter's diapers, not even once ...

Nasio (1990) wrote: "I believe, in effect, that men who—perhaps painfully—recognize their own feminine aspect are more able to accept their difficult role as father than those who do not recognize their femininity." Ivan perceived that his conflicts kept him from exercising the paternal function.

A: [I ask for associations to the dream]

Ivan: "The little blonde had straight hair ... oops! my little girl is blonde ... I hope I don't have a whore for a daughter ... My sister also is blonde. And I know a little whore who's studying now and got engaged ... it's been a while since she's fucked ... She looked like a schoolgirl the other day when she came into my shop with her fiancé ... My other friend also fucks her. That's life. And she's all serious with this guy, just to think that we used to have these great parties and cock sucks ... she's beautiful."

As I have pointed out, his narrative tends to go from "whore" to "death". This was indeed the case here.

Ivan went on: "I've started over again from zero ... I feel anxious that something's going to happen to me ... something to do with death ... I get scared and on the other hand I couldn't give a shit ... I still don't know what I want out of life ... Maybe I want to die ... I don't know ... I'm not a woman ..."

A: "Maybe you would have liked to be born a woman."

Ivan: "I've got to change this way of being ... I when I was little I used to put on my mother's under-slip when I was starting to jerk off ... My old lady's under-slip was white, with shiny straps and I used to put it on, get up onto a pillow and jerk off ... sometimes I'd use her underpants ... And one thing I'd forgotten, my sister's big doll, I'd take it with me ... sometimes I'd put the finger in my ass and come ... I like whores to suck my ass and put just the tip of their tongue in ... a lot of guys don't like that ... they get mad ... ha, ha [he laughs, nervous and anxious] ... Ivana [he says the feminine version of his name]. Dad preferred my sister."

A: "If you'd been born a girl, your father would have paid more attention to you."

Ivan: [agrees tearfully] "Yes ... her eyes are blue like his ... that's the reason for my machismo, my anxiety, what connection can you find there?"

A: "If dad won't love me as a boy, I prefer to die."

Ivan: "And how can you fix that? I wish! I wish it could change! I had obliterated all this ... I don't know how we got it out, with the whore who sucked my cock, I don't know [he refers to material we worked on in a previous session] ... I'm really hung up over all this ..."

In the transference, I function both as an organizing father and as the person who introduces the enigmatic feminine element whose presence he rejects.

Sometimes I am included in his body language from the homosexual angle. "You've already put your finger up my ass several times."

As the analysis runs its course, intrapsychic symbolization takes place, and his compulsions begin to loosen up.

When he begins to feel more clearly identified as masculine, he is less desirous of pushing away his feminine components and less ashamed to perform activities that are supposed to be the exclusive concern of women (he likes to cook and take his children to the park).

Two erotic transference dreams in the final part of his analysis represented a milestone. They announced the coming together of the two currents, erotic and tender. After that, Ivan was able to "make love", something new that made him both ashamed and frightened. Up till then, he had always "had sex", in an attempt to reaffirm his phallic position in the encounter between two bodies and to expel any tenderness. The figure of the prostitute was in the service of this kind of splitting, and with his wife he found it impossible to be tender when eroticism was involved.

This is his first dream:

I was in bed, covered up. You were next to me and suddenly, you jumped on me and rubbed my head, tenderly, you touched my head and my neck, it was nice, if was as if you were my old lady. It scared me a bit.

I interpreted that our heads seemed to be making love. During the session, Ivan said: "I feel I'm getting better and my outlook on life is more positive, I realize what I'm doing, sometimes even I can't believe I did it."

The second dream was intensely erotic:

> I was in bed with you, I was fucking you, you were wearing black lace underwear, you had a lot of make-up on, I sucked you all over, all the erogenous zones.

He associated black lace to a black widow (hence the idea of a man dying). I felt that this dream forecasted the end of Ivan's analysis. In processing these elements, the split-off erotic currents were becoming integrated, and soon afterwards, Ivan talked about important changes to intimate aspects of his married life, as well as a gradual loss of interest in seeking out other women.

Conclusions

My aim in this paper is to show how a male patient's conflicts involving his feminine aspects derived from difficulties in resolving the Oedipus complex. When he had to face up to his femininity, Ivan felt he had to humiliate himself. In the grip of intense anxiety, he sought refuge in a sterile kind of machismo that, though it gave him some degree of pleasure, highlighted the deep suffering behind the compulsive quality of his masculine exploits.

For men, the "bedrock" is the repudiation of femininity. At best, they can come close to it and recognize the variety of meanings inherent in it. I have described these features above: weakness, inferiority, mystery, life and death ... By working through fears of castration and consolidating the passage from imaginary castration to symbolic castration (Lacan, 1958), it becomes possible for men to integrate feminine elements, diminishing negative oedipal anxieties and reaffirming masculinity.

Every psychic envelope is bisexual (D. Anzieu, personal communication, February, 1991). Accepting and struggling with both components of this envelope is fundamental for access to good psychic functioning. The rejection of the purely feminine envelope generates symptoms—in Ivan, for example, it drifted towards a strong attraction to phallic women (he included his wife in this category), while totally denigrating women supposedly placed in feminine positions. Essentially, his anxiety had its roots in an identification with a feminine image and the free rein he gave to negative oedipal fantasies. With his "excessive overcompensation" he created an infantile and clownish hyper-virile feminine image to alleviate his anxiety.

Ivan's analysis gave me access to the feminine–masculine vicissitudes to which this male patient found himself subjected, as well as enabling me to approach his bedrock. Initial "repudiation of femininity" turned into a milder "refusal" that involved more integration and acceptance of his bisexuality.

Notes

1. This paper has been published in Spanish in 1994 under the title "El hombre y su roca viva: rehusarse a la femineidad" in Mujeres por Mujeres, Biblioteca Peruana de Psicoanálisis, Moisés Lemlij editor, pp. 182–193.
2. I am grateful to the psychoanalytic German-speaking group of the Argentine Psychoanalytic Association, and especially to Marcelo Aptekmann, for advising me of this nuance of translation.

CHAPTER THREE

What do men want?[1]

Jacqueline Amati Mehler

M any years ago, when feminism was at its height, a friend of mine, who was very sympathetic towards the women's movement, said "very soon my fellow men will react and organize something like a *'Man's Syndicate'*!" However, a man's syndicate was not constituted, but what did occur was the flourishing of a vast "crisis literature"—especially in the USA—on male identity. Some authors, in reaction to feminist critique, tried to vindicate masculinity while others attempted to claim that men were more exploited than women. Many men, however, reacted to feminist critique with a serious revision of their own traditional gender values. While a lot has been written about women's subordination and exploitation and about women's sexual liberation, very few authors (some sociologists, many journalists, but almost no analysts) have attempted to explore the intimate and deep changes that the sexual liberation of women has brought about in the intimate relationship between men and women.

In an article entitled "What do men want?", Richard A. Shweder (1994) gives an accurate review of the so-called male identity crisis literature and speaks of it "... as a long delayed response to twenty years of feminist critique". Most of these publications have a psycho-social ideological approach to debating whether males and females are alike or whether they are different and, in this case, to the discussion of the main differences. Some more sophisticated writers analyse the image of one or the other gender in myths and different cultures and they give a phenomenological description of current changes in the male–female relationship. Many predict, as an outcome of a self-examining conscience, a "new male" at this *"Time of Fallen Heroes"* (the title of a book by Betcher and Pollack, 1993). Meanwhile, Kathleen Gerson from New York University, who did an extensive sociological survey, documents an increasing class of "autonomous" males who, concluding that it is too burdensome and time consuming to oppress, protect or cooperate with the other sex, prefer to avoid entanglements with women and to live alone.

Issues of nature (anatomy, neurology, genetics, hormones, etc) versus culture are, of course, at the centre of more "scientific" arguments but, be it as it is, the shared view is that something different is inhabiting the field of male–female interactions. It is this aspect that has intruded into my clinical understanding of some of the classical sexual problems of our patients.[2]

Among these, chance led me to pay particular attention to the problems of male sexuality, especially male impotence, because I encounter this problem more frequently now than in the earlier days of my clinical practice. I became particularly interested in its relation to love and to object relations and I was struck by how little literature there is on this subject. I felt that the developments in psychoanalytic knowledge of earlier psychic processes allowed for the understanding of this syndrome under a more complex perspective. I have discussed elsewhere (1992), with abundant clinical material, the question of male impotence in relation to the issue of separation–individuation, as it displays itself in the transference–counter-transference interaction. Whereas my attention had primarily focused, in individual cases, on the relation between the vicissitudes of the early phase of symbiotic indifferentiation and its connection with the clinical manifestation of impotence within a heterosexual love relation, I have lately started to wonder more often about the impact of the current generalized social and cultural tendency towards sexual indifferentiation on the fate of individual identity, its role in child development and in interpersonal heterosexual relations. Unisex—if I may use a more or less wild analogy—seems to have become equivalent to *"egalite, liberte, fraternite"* and I think that a dramatic confusion is taking place between socio-ideological levels, on one hand, and psychological levels, on the other. To those who claim that man and women differ very little at the level of psychosexual development I would like to recall another famous French phrase (albeit rejecting its original discriminatory meaning!) that says: *"vive la petite difference"*! The Gay anti-discrimination campaign has promoted socio-cultural changes leading to the quite recent recognition by the European Community of homosexual marriage and the recommendation that these couples be granted the right to adopt children. This step deserves thorough discussion in all its complex human, legal, and sociological aspects. However, entering that field would require still another paper. I would only like to call attention now to what appears to me as being an irreversible, slow, trend towards non-differentiation that, I'm afraid, might—at least partly—derive from a misunderstanding of psychological tenets in relation to family interactions and to ways of child-rearing practices. I believe that, nowadays, nobody would object to men sharing what used to be "feminine tasks", or to fathers sharing childcare. In analysis, we have also become more subtle in distinguishing between father and mother, as male and female, and "maternal" or "paternal" as being interchangeable functions.

However, I cannot help wondering about the effect of further steps taken in the direction of total confusion between mother and father. To illustrate my point I shall describe an example that I have recently observed of "advanced" childcare counselling in the feeding of newborn babies.

In special cases of mothers who, initially, do not have enough milk to feed their babies, and/or of babies who do not suck sufficiently, the extra milk pumped from the mother's breasts in-between feeds is put into a special bottle that has two thin tubes coming out of the lid from which the milk can flow. During breast feeding, the mother tapes the tubes to her nipples so that the baby sucks from both nipple and tubes, thus achieving stimulation of the breast milk as well as reducing the child's frustration. When the mother is resting or working and the father feeds the baby, rather than using a plain feeding bottle with a teat, he does so with this same special bottle containing the milk pumped from the mother's breast. In order to provide the baby with an experience as close as possible to having mother's nipple in the mouth, *father is advised* to tape the two tubes to his finger and to then introduce it into the baby's mouth, who sucks the finger together with the milk flowing from the tubes. (I shall abstain from confessing my own perverse phantasies when I saw this.) We could ask, of course, what is to prevent the further step of father taping the tubes to his own nipple, in the same way as the mother. Besides consequences to the child's capacity to differentiate father from mother, and him or herself from the two different primary objects (about which we can only speculate), I think we could wonder about such medical advice and its connection to man's deep unconscious envy of maternal functions disguised by shared parenthood responsibilities.

Let me go back now to the point from which my reflections started, namely to the attempt to understand the underlying vicissitudes of male impotence. Most literature dealing with masculine impotence views this disturbance in relation to castration anxiety, or like M. Klein (1946) and her followers, to early anxieties connected with phantasies of ... "attacking and sadistically entering the mother's body ... which would also contain father's penis, and lead to the dread of mother herself". Although classical Freudian formulations, relating impotence to the fixation to incestuous phantasies, retain all their validity, in my mind two questions require further attention. Firstly, I think that *there are many different forms of impotence*: we are dealing with a symptom rather than with a specific psychopathological entity. Secondly, I believe that what has not been sufficiently attended to is the contribution that knowledge of *earlier processes of psychic development* can make for a better understanding of sexual impotence.

I have tried to integrate, in my understanding of impotence, the knowledge derived from earlier phases of development in which the self and the object are fused and undifferentiated. I would hope that this could also help us to a better understanding of the changes that I mentioned above, in the sense of the effects of what I think is a widespread standardized blurring of gender differences. (This is also perhaps amplified by a general socio-cultural tendency that penalizes individuality.)

In "A special type of choice of object made by men" Freud (1910a) describes ways in which neurotic men behave in love:

enacting the tendency to make an engaged women the object of their love and thus gratifying impulses of rivalry and hostility connected with the oedipal situation; experiencing conscious and unconscious conflict between the choice of either an idealized and highly valued woman, or of a debased prostitute-like surrogate of the "instinctual" mother. In "On the universal tendency to debasement in the sphere of love", Freud gives perhaps his most explicit contribution to the understanding of masculine impotence. He claims that:

> ... foundation of the disorder is provided by an inhibition in the developmental history of the libido before it assumes the form which we take to be its normal termination ... An incestuous fixation ... plays a predominant part in this pathogenic material and is its most universal content ... Two currents, whose union is necessary to ensure a completely normal attitude in love have, in the cases we are considering, failed to combine. These two may be distinguished as the affectionate and the sensual current. [Freud, 1912, p. 180]

When affection and sensuality are not linked but opposed, due to fixation to incestuous phantasies, the capacity to love will be marked by this split. "Restriction has thus been placed on object choice" (Freud, 1912, p. 182). The affectionate sensual current and the sexual wish can only seek gratification from two different objects, since fusion of both currents has failed.

Long-standing social conventions which considered it normal for a man to have extramarital affairs, allowed—with minimum conflict—for this internal scenario to be syntonic with external reality. Moreover, a widespread conception of manhood, confirmed through permanent conquest of sexual objects, allows for the reinforcement of defensive splitting of the object choice. A patient of mine, who had continuous affairs but happened to become very involved with one particular woman from whom he couldn't part, came around to considering both his wife and his lover as being in a different category from all the rest of the women. He felt that all his other numerous interchangeable erotic objects were just "prostitute-like little sensual animals".

While Freud uses the terms "sexual" and "sensual" as synonyms, I think it is important to differentiate these two components in order to deepen our understanding of love and its vicissitudes, impotence among them.

Sensuality, as I am viewing it here, is connected with pleasure provided by sense organs which, starting in the infant from non-differentiated auto-sensual-eroticism moves, via transitional activities, towards the integration of sensations within the self-object dialogical vicissitudes. Sexuality in its more mature, genital expressions includes sensuality as the earliest phases of "affection", but entails the emergence of object aimed libidinal and aggressive drives.

What, in my mind, has been neglected is that which may be impossible to integrate *within the same relation*, not only affection and sexuality, as described by Freud, but also—and perhaps even primarily—*the merging of fusional and genital levels* of experience, both being intrinsic and essential parts of love and intercourse. What appears to be extremely threatening regards the implied degree of regression at various levels, for such experiences to coexist. Here, I make a distinction between a tender affection carrying a sensual stream, linked to a regressive fusional experience, and a different kind of affection which does not prevalently involve such merging experiences. The first one, marked by early concrete bodily experiences, can be resumed in all its infantile polymorphism (albeit fused with genitality) in the service of love and mature sexuality.

It thus follows that I am referring to two different kinds of vicissitudes within the "coexistence" of affection and sexuality. One regards the object choice (idealized or debased), bearing on and manifesting itself along *interpersonal* lines. The other regards the *intrapsychic* capacity to bear regression and deliver oneself, with the same object in shared passion and genital love, to the most primary erotic affection, embedded in the "oceanic" totalizing symbiotic experience that lacks boundaries between self and object. Disturbances of either kind of "coexistence" of affection and sexuality—whether regarding object choice or the capacity for deep intimate closeness with the object, at different levels—can be variably organized in normal life and in neurosis, confronting us with varying and compound conditions of impotence, according to the eventual admixture with other neurotic components.

In some cases we are dealing with total impotence, due to lack or inhibition of desire. For such men this condition is independent of a real available object and depends on their own faithful libidinal allegiance to the unconscious incestuous (prohibited) object.

In other cases we find a selective impotence, so well described by Freud when dealing with the case of men who, impotent with an idealized mother figure, can have "normal" intercourse with devalued, debased, "instinctual-like" mother surrogates. Sometimes these men may run into total, frightening, impotence when they are sexually involved with a partner who, appearing initially as a superficial affair, is liable to become more than the object of a split sexual investment. The temporary fall of defences renders the liaison a threatening source of haunting, infantile, incestuous phantasies. A compromise situation may be set up, whereby a partial debasement of the object (considered "just" a sexual object) and a constant phobic-like attitude, maintaining the object neither too close nor too detached, can represent an attempt to grant survival to such a relationship if it meets the object's implicit collusion.

Among those particular instances that account for intermittent or occasional impotence—increasingly frequent in our practice—we come across men who have hitherto functioned well, engaging in more or less free, affectionate or stable relations, but who, upon falling deeply in love, are unable to have intercourse with their new partner and react with intense anxiety and despair to such a paradoxical situation. It is precisely the perception of a major involvement, more intense, or "different" from previous ones that is frightening and felt as a threat to their usual internal set up and stability.

Other men can function sexually well with their life partner—who may often be frigid or unresponsive—while they run into incipient states of transitory impotence if involved with sexually responsive partners. As mentioned above, the crisis of impotence coincides with the highest peak of desire and simultaneous defence from closeness.[3]

I think that cases of covert potential impotence are more frequently uncovered today by virtue of the changes in social and sexual habits following women's emancipation. More freedom and a decrease of sexual inhibition have implications, both in the cases of men who tend to make split object choices, and in those who fear intimacy and merging experiences with the object. As I commented before, in the traditional set-up (when separation and divorce were unusual), it was natural and standard for men to entertain multiple sexual relations (while remaining attached to a non sexualized mother-like central figure). This enhanced and allowed for a "physiological" split of object-roles, as described by Freud. While this is still ongoing current practice, I believe that fewer women are ready to view themselves as doomed to social shame if they start an affair with an engaged man, or to irreparably submit to being forever a "second—or secondary—object" with a man ready to entertain a split double object choice. This is probably contributing to confront men with more demanding partners.

On the other hand, we see nowadays many young men who, confronted with an increasing number of independent women who fall less easily into the categories or roles of the "idealized" or "debased" sexual object, are very worried about their manhood when a love relation comes up. Others tend to entertain mainly non-differentiated friendly "sibling-like" symbiotic relations—often including sex, but with hardly any passion or that particular quality that pertains to feelings of encountering a "special" object.

There seems to be a fairly widespread belief that women seek and tolerate fusional levels in love more than men who, as I have described above, can run into sexual *defaillances* when confronted with fearful regressive trends. Is this true? And if so, why? While clinical evidence makes me side with those who believe that this is true, it is hard to formulate convincing theoretical explanations to justify it. I can think of a few; but objections to any of them are not that easy to defeat. I am perfectly aware, furthermore, that many analysts have clinical evidence to prove that women can have as much difficulty as men in experiencing closeness and merging; and with very sound arguments as well, such as the fact that while men cannot conceal sexual *defaillance* to themselves or their partners, women can feel and convey authentic participation to their partners whilst being uncertain as to whether they achieved orgasm or not. While this is undeniable, we could still argue that, for most men, the lack of erection or orgasm will be (consciously) experienced as equivalent to not making love, whilst for many women this is not the case at all, and the affectionate sensual foreplay can be felt as gratifying in its own right.

Freud used the term symbiosis when referring to the "oceanic sense" (letter to Romain Rolland in 1930, p. 67) as a "feeling of an indissoluble bond, of being one with the external world as a whole".

He also refers to the state of being in love when, at its height, the boundary between ego and object threatens to melt away, as the adult version of an infantile feeling of the self, when: "the infant does not as yet distinguish his ego from the external world as the source of the sensations flowing in upon him".

It is my view that individual capacity to feel the full range of merging and emerging experiences in intercourse, within a love relation, will be marked by the way in which the process of differentiation between self and object has taken place. It is precisely the intricate separation–individuation processes, within the complex interweaving of regressive symbiotic trends, as opposed to differentiation—*with its necessary quota of aggressive drives in the service of growth*—that may fall short of a sufficiently adequate outcome in terms of permeable self-object boundaries. Here, we are dealing with the defence of regressive fusional experience.

A crucial issue that needs to be further explored is the problem of aggression underlying male impotence. The cases of occasional impotence that I came across within my practice (certainly not sufficient to allow for generalizations) involved men who had healthy competitive drives at the service of work and personal achievement, while they were extremely passive and submissive with their regular partners.

This subject introduced, in the analysis of X, an impotent patient (Amati Mehler, 1992), the theme of passive compliance with parental wishes at the cost of not recognizing his own except in regard to his professional development. X was deeply attached to his parents who had a very symbiotic relation between them and with their son. He was able to defy his father, who would always warn him against striving for what appeared difficult or unrealistic professional goals, by achieving very successful intellectual and business enterprises. The patient's need to challenge whatever the father felt to be impossible, on the one hand inflated his omnipotence, but on the other it allowed him to achieve a partial release from an engulfing symbiosis that involved not only him and his mother but also the father, enhancing an even more generalized confusion of self-object boundaries and differentiated identifications. Seduction coupled with compliance had a considerable impact on the management of frustration and aggression in his relation with his wife and other women, with whom he entertained multiple affairs. But the anger that he roused in his partners, as well as the anger experienced by two women patients of mine over the repeated failure of their love partners, made me wonder. These two women, otherwise sympathetic and understanding, after sharing exciting foreplay with their partners whose erection dropped right before penetration, felt this *defaillance* as a betrayal and an attack on the relationship. They felt that their partners would bring them along to a state of blissful abandonment and then—as one of them said—she would be left alone and without containment at the time when she felt that she was totally "losing herself". The subjective experience of these female patients corresponded to, and mirrored, their partners' difficulty in letting themselves go, lose control of the situation, and share the sense of loss of boundaries. But what was more relevant was that there was the perception of a sort of miscarriage or displacement of the aggressive drive rather than it remaining in the service of attachment and bonding intimacy through penetration.

If we agree that the pathway of our "becoming" a more or less separate individual with his/her own identity is embedded within an interpersonal–relational matrix, and if we accept that our subjectivity contains the indelible traces of our internal (representational) self-objects' interaction, then we can more readily understand how each encounter, in its dialogic interaction, is liable to arouse different levels of response, potential growth or defensive retreat within ourselves. From this angle then, a deep involving love relation that has the potential to enhance a vast scale of sharing experiences—ranging from the most archaic regressive and fusional quality (bodily and psychological) to all other evolving forms of deep psychological and intellectual involvement—is doomed to meet the bedrock of individual capacity for experimenting with complete intimacy. This capacity is then related, in its deepest layers, to those processes which, engendered along the development of separation–individuation processes, lead to gender identity, thus allowing not only to recognize the "other", but also to identify with the "different" other. This is of the utmost importance if the merging experience in love, with the blurring of ego boundaries, is not to overlap with the earlier frightening and annihilating aspects of the sense of loss of the self, or to induce anxieties about one's own "maleness" or "femininity".

In a paper on gender identity, Argentieri (1990) remarks that "anatomy (or biology) is not destiny and is not in itself sufficient to guarantee adequate drive development or specific gender identity". Although one could hardly disagree with it, it is still important to detect whether and when *anatomy, in its mental representation and fantasies,* may determine the modality in which faulty processes of separation–individuation influence drive development and sexual life.

Ferenczi (1923) considers intercourse as a partial regression to intrauterine life and wrote: "the male penetrates the female genital with his penis, which is a miniature representation of the ego ..." I would like to point here to *the penis as the infantile version of the ego,* because in my view it illustrates some of the clinical situations to which I am referring.

In a paper entitled "The body as phallus: a patient's fear of erection" Sandler (1959) describes a patient who, like X, was exposed to intense sexual stimulation from his mother, experienced at a phallic level. This excitement, in both its defensive and positive expression, led to his whole body "being phallicized". On one hand, the patient's body was rigid and immobile to prevent erection and on the other, several somatic reactions (blushing, stiff-neck, etc) evidenced the body–phallus equation.

This "phallus–body" equation, at a phallic level, also showed its defensive aspect (from castration) in my patient Mr X who had the feeling that, when erected, his penis did not belong to him. At a deeper than phallic level though, a more regressive form of this equation was clearly expressed in the following dream of my patient:

> I was in a place of thermal baths, a place a bit like a clinic, maybe for old people. The whole place was fenced and access to it was underground. It had a fantastic park and was a lovely place [the search for the lost *"infantile paradise"* had been a leitmotif in previous sessions] and I was with a woman, don't know who. I looked through the window, inside the pavilions, and saw many naked women, white and plump, lying down with their little children. They are ill and it seems as if they could be disassembled, like, say, if you had a kidney that didn't work it would be dismantled, set to their side and remain connected to them—as if it were an artificial kidney or one in dialysis. But I wasn't sure if it was

their organs or their children that were lying aside ... I say to myself
that probably those are their organs and they do not work properly
... Even if it's not a bloody situation, I think it's horrible.

This oneiric image—from which this patient could not make out
whether what lay close to the mothers' bodies were penises,
mothers' organs or babies—seems to me to illustrate precisely the
core issue of what symbiotic, merging experience represents for the
cases that I am trying to illustrate. On one hand, it represents the
wish to regain the "lost paradise" of complete reunion with the
primary object, separation from which threatens survival and
constitutes ... "the prototype of all castration", as Freud (1909a)
points out in a footnote, added in 1926, to the case of "Little Hans".
On the other hand, at a very deep level, the claustrophobic-like
phantasies reveal fears related to the penis carrying along with it,
during intercourse, all the body-self inside a woman, and concretely
remaining a "hostage" inside a woman's body just as a part of
himself—in the case of this patient—had remained a psychological
hostage of his mother.

Coming back to the relation between anatomy (or biology) and
destiny, and to the debated question of whether women tolerate
more than men the fusional levels in love, whatever the fear of
closeness or merging experience may represent for them, the
underlying symbiotic phantasies in which the anxiety is embedded,
inasmuch as they are intimately connected to the mental representation of early body–mind interactions, could hardly be the same as
those of men. A further complication is that part of the symbiotic tie
of the little girl is carried over from the mother to the father,
enhancing its longer duration as well as implying a difference in the
process of retroactive re-signification (*Nachtraglichkeit*) of early
anxieties in relation to the primary objects. So, while women are
bound to a much more difficult process of primary disidentification
with the mother, a quota of fusional experience will physiologically
"survive" the separation from her through normal investment in
the father and male objects. Men may relinquish primary
identification and fusion with the mother more easily through
identification with the father, but regressive merging experiences,
during intercourse with a woman, can always risk bringing them
closer to indifferentiation in which the fear of total reingulfment

(A. Freud, 1952) is reactivated. In fact, as I wrote elsewhere, impotence can be the herald of a great passionate love, but, paradoxically—as a last resort for survival—the fear of regression can also defeat love.

To conclude, we may wonder, what the opposite situation would entail, when no regression is feared—or even feasible—because there simply has been little differentiation, and diversity rather than valued, is losing its socio-cultural sense. I am not only wondering about the possible effects of this general maternal–paternal and male–female functional overlap on our theories. I am rather concerned, on one hand, with issues of gender identity from an individual developmental viewpoint; and, on the other hand, it is hard not to wonder about the fate of male and female gender interactions, especially concerning *attraction* towards the "other" as separate and different. No difference implies no tension, but rather a narcissistic mirroring oneself in the "same–other".

What will be the fate of *desire*, curiosity and the wish to penetrate the mysteries of the unknown Other in the search for mature genital object love?

Notes

1. This paper "Qué quieren los hombres" has been published in Spanish in 1994 in M. Lemlij (Ed.), *Mujeres por Mujeres*, Biblioteca peruana de Psicoanálisis, Lima, pp. 134–145.
2. I will not dwell here on the controversial debate about whether women have really achieved autonomy and sexual liberation or, whether men have really changed their behaviour towards women over the last decade. Certainly this controversy could be contextualized within more precise data regarding different cultures or age groups and the result of such research could eventually modify the perspective of some of my own assumptions. However, my present discussion is merely based on clinical observations derived from my experience with male and female patients over the last years.
3. Other forms of impotence manifest themselves through premature ejaculation or protracted erection with anorgasmia.

CHAPTER FOUR

Male sexuality and mental void

Jaime M. Lutenberg

Introduction

T hroughout his work, Freud gave sexuality a particular role, on which he based his whole theory. The complex difference between child and adult sexuality was drawn out of the concept of "drive". The revolution generated on this premise, gave way to the following one hundred years of theory and practice of psychoanalysis. The interruption of a patient's associative flow during the session, was one of the mysteries that surprised Freud. From this derived in his theoretical conceptualization of repression, resistance, and transference.

According to my experience, when many of the patients consulting nowadays remain silent during the session, they are simultaneously giving evidence of two different phenomena: (a) sometimes silence is directly derived from repression; or (b) silence is derived from the underlying mental void; there is nothing but a void behind the silence. The clinical difference between these phenomena is significant and leads to very different technical approaches.

In recent years, there has been an increase of consultations on borderline pathology, combined with drug-addiction, complex and polymorphous cases of "neosexuality" (McDougall, 1991), and cases of severe anorexia. I understand that mental void is nuclear in all of these cases. It is made evident, during analysis, that the nuclear disturbance does not only refer to the intrapsychic flow of mental contents (unconscious representation, preconscient, unconscious phantasy), but also to the alteration of the mind used as "container" of the referred "contents". We can see, in each session, the complicated disturbances in the container–contained link (Bion, 1970), so typical of mental void.

In male patients having severe problems in the nucleus of their narcissistic structure, disturbed sexuality is an attempt at compensating for mental void and not a mere manifestation of "perversion". Through their multifaceted factual sexuality, these people try to generate, in their ego, the conviction that they are "super-men", but they never become wholly convinced of this. I believe these are cases of narcissistic fragility, primarily originated in defensive symbiotic bounds, reproduced in adult life. In these patients, all kinds of sexual disorders represent a defence against mental void. They make use of the "Don Juan" behaviour in a compulsive style, so as to enclose and/or eject the void experienced in their sexual "objects".

The dynamic link between mental void and sexuality can be understood only if we accept the possibility of a personality with different ego split portions, there being no contact among those parts. Such structural ego split portions are generated by psychic "abortions" suffered during their personal evolutive life story. This is generally the case with patients having severe problems with their paternal identification, combined with a symbiotic link to their mothers.

After a vignette, I will make reference to the theoretical hypotheses that support these assertions.

Vignette

Andrew consults after an accident he had three months ago. He ran into a car while riding his motorcycle. He feels responsible for the accident. He says: "I was careless". He broke his left arm and had problems in his wrist. He says: "My girl-friend insisted that I should come and gave me your telephone number". During his interview, he also mentions he has problems at work and suffers great tension. He is a broker and is connected with the financial world. He lives alone.

Regarding his sexual life, he says he does not feel he is under real obligation to his girlfriend. However, they have satisfactory sexual intercourse. At the same time, he has sex with other girls that he occasionally meets. He just sees them once or twice. These encounters are characterized by contempt and brevity. Andrew says that he is only interested in evacuating sensations derived from his "sexual requirements" and not in any kind of feeling or emotion.

Mixed up with these "sexual requirements", I also detected that he made evident a certain disagreeable sensation, present at other different moments. It was a kind of sensation of futility, just as if his life had no sense. When he got home, he suddenly felt reluctant or unwilling to do things. Anything he did, he felt was useless or had no sense. So he would wander about in his car or motorbike. He turned into a sort of senseless robot. Everything he had, got like blurred, as if detached from his existence. He would quickly pass from a feeling of loneliness to the "feeling of nothingness".

It was under these circumstances that he searched for a sexual partenaire, an unknown woman, that he called "his victim". He was not anxious, but bored and without sense. Going deeper into what he would call "boredom", I inferred his sensation of mental void. It is important to differentiate this from boredom or from what patients call "depression". It is an altogether different feeling.

By going out during the night, he also tried to hide his unbearable insomnia, which he otherwise solved with specific medication. I realized he would panic when he felt he was about to fall asleep, so he would not sleep. Many other concomitant factors led me to infer that it was very easy for him to pass from the signal of anxiety to terror. There appeared, during the sessions, reports of terror-filled dreams, in which he felt he was falling, due to different reasons.

I am going to transcribe the beginning of a session, after six months of treatment. He has three sessions a week. This is a Wednesday session. He most generally sits down on the couch, he rarely lies down. This kind of flexibility is indispensable with these patients.

He is ten-minutes late. He lies down on the couch, then he sits up, he looks at me, he yawns and lies down again; he rubs his eyes, unbuttons his shirt cuffs and sighs. [In my counter-transference, I perceive a contrast between his childlike fragility, shown in connection with the beginning of a session and his formal look: suit, long-sleeved shirt, tie. When he unbuttons his long-sleeved shirt cuffs, I feel he is trying to sort of "decompress" himself, although it is not simple for him to do so.] He sits up and starts talking.

P: "You know what? But listen ... I can't find the words. I've been having several dreams, and I am in ..., how to tell you ..., a dangerous situation. In my dream, my life is in danger. But I realize it is a dream, while dreaming it. In my dream, I was up on a pyramid and I had a bicycle and I was riding down and when I was about to fall, to collapse, to have a free fall, then I woke up. I was at the top of the pyramid, and the father of the girl I met the other day told me I had to go down, and I didn't know how. So I thrust myself down with the bicycle and then a strong anxiety overcame me, seeing that I was having a free fall. I realized it was a dream. The most important thing is that there emerged from me a big inner force, telling me it was a dream, and I woke up. And this is important to me. I don't care about the rest."

This pendular movement of sitting up and lying down is characteristic of these patients. Far from giving evidence of fear of analysis due to resistance (like in neuroses), these patients bear such a psychic fragility that they, easily and without control, can shift from signal anxiety (neurotic part) to terror (psychotic part, following Bion).

This patient makes particular movements with his body before producing verbal associations. I call these movements "free body associations" (Lutenberg, 1993). They are linked to his difficulty in beginning his report and thus revive those emotions proper of the terrifying scene of his "nightmare". As we can see, his oneiric images (losing control of his bicycle) also lead us to his accidents with his motorbike.

Many accidents of this type correspond to actual unconscious suicide attempts. In those people with mental void, these are not manifestations of melancholia or schizophrenia, but real attempts of killing the "alive" dead they carry inside; this "invisible dead" corresponds to their mental void. It becomes evident with any object separation experienced by the subject.

As shown by the threat of a free fall down the pyramid, he is afraid of "falling" (regression) off his ego without control. This type of dream is the updating of many others the patient had in his childhood. He used to feel he was in a whirlpool, falling together with some of his toys; sometimes he would wake up out of anxiety, others because he actually fell down from bed.

The presence of a "father" in the dream is very important, this man telling him to throw himself down the pyramid in free fall. It is not possible for me now to discuss the relationship between the feeling of guilt born with the Oedipus complex, experienced by a part of his ego, and the feeling of collapsing, experienced by the other part. We can also witness the appearance of a kind of anxiety that Winnicott named "Fear of Breakdown" (1982).

But for Andrew, the most significant element of the dream was the fact that he came out safe and sound—in the explicit content itself—that he was able to realize it was a dream, differentiating it from a magic premonition, at the same time differentiating it from reality; he confounds both levels again when considering his oneiric "salvation" as something real.

I understand this is referring to his unconscious suicide attempts; he calms down when perceiving there is a firm disposition of his ego to prevent such a fatal ending. During his adolescence, he used to have this tendency to "having accidents", as well as to drugs. In reference to this point, there is another question to be considered: his sexual behaviour and AIDS danger.

After having analysed some of the phantasies connected with his dream, he added: "In my dream, the bicycle had a gearbox, but not the one bikes usually have. It was attached to the handlebar, like in motorbikes. I would really like to ride a motorbike now, but you see, how could I possibly do it, dressed as I am, in a suit, wearing a tie and all that. I should be wearing a black jacket, boots and leather trousers, like in the dream."

I understood he was talking about a present differentiation, about different identities. But, on the other hand, after feeling more reassured, he was trying to differentiate the oneiric phenomenon from an instance of hallucination, lived during the night.

Theoretical approach

The complexity of the sexual life of some patients is not primarily caused by the "acting-out" generated by their instinctive, pregenital fixations (Freud, 1905, 1923, 1924) or polymorphous and/or perverse fixations (Meltzer, 1973), but by an attempt of (defensive) compensation of the underlying mental void.

It is through their polymorphous sexual life that they try to hide or to overcome, depending on the case, their mental void and its underlying emotion—terror. Their sexual behaviour can also be originated in an attempt of evolution emerged from the split parts of their personality. (I am here making reference to the non-integrated areas of the split ego.)

Patients with mental void have a tendency to pass from the signal of anxiety to dread. This is an indication of their ego fragility, particularly the narcissistic fragility of the organizing identifications of their psychic apparatus. This situation renders them vulnerable to regression in transference.

They are fragile to the feeling of frustration emerging from the rules of the analytical setting. They are not always able to recover, from the point of view of their ego structural strength, after regression experienced during the session. Their dependence is usually split and placed in polymorphous or perverse sexual links. Their dependence is generally of the symbiotic type (Bleger, 1967), although during analysis, a more developed transference may appear, proper of the oedipal or pre-oedipal sexuality.

This type of transference is a clear indication of the permanent unstable equilibrium these people have between the most developed aspects of their ego and the complexities of their archaic psyche, which remains split from the rest of their personality. The split portion of the ego and the repressed portion of the ego are very different, when considering psychic quality.

The clinical complexity of such kaleidoscopic personalities can only be understood, from the theoretical point of view, if we admit that their ego is split into several parts, none of which is in contact with the other or among themselves. This is the reason why it is so difficult for them to achieve the ego synthesis of the lived experience.

From Freud onwards, frustration is the starting point of the ego elaborative demand. Neurotic defence is typical of neurosis.

Psychotic defence leads the ego to produce massive projective identification. Hallucination is thus generated with the aim of placing the absent object in the perceptual field (Bion, 1967–1970). Symbiotic defence cancels psychic pain generated by the conscientious object loss. It works by means of object substitution and secondary fusion with the replacing object.

Several writers speak of a period of normal symbiosis (Bleger, 1967; Mahler, 1967, 1984). When different problems affect mother–baby separation, not only a "fixing" process occurs, following Freud, but there also appears a secondary symbiotic defence, different from the original symbiosis, which is due to evolution and non-pathological.

The secondary symbiotic defence holds the link in equilibrium. When this link is broken up, there appears a feeling of dread (Freud, 1926a) or of breakdown (Winnicott, 1982) or nameless dread (Bion, 1967). All repetitions (compulsion of repetition) generated by the break up of this symbiotic defence occur under the logics of "Beyond the Pleasure Principle", following Freud (1920b).

When we face clinical facts, the repetition of which is explained by the logics of the pleasure principle, we can infer that it is not an instinctual discharge that we expect through each repetition, but an instinctual "cathexis", the one generated by the psychic inscription of the drive. It is the origin of a "cathexis presentation", organizer of the unconscious system.

The analysis of children and of psychotic patients (Klein, 1957; Bion, 1965, 1967, 1970; Rosenfeld, 1965; Meltzer, 1973; Searles, 1980; Winnicott, 1982) and the experience gained with baby observation (M. Mahler), made it possible for a number of post-Freudian thinkers to start new trends in the analysis of patients who, during their analytic regression, present atypical situations. Particularly, the hypotheses of Bleger (1967), Green (1990, 1999, 2001), Tustin (1972, 1981, 1990) and Anzieu (1985), helped me to understand better the concept of dread used by Freud in his work, and then, the concept of mental void.

Summarizing my personal synthesis, born out of the different theories of these authors, and articulating this with the hypotheses of the first and second Freudian topics, we can conceive that the split ego (Freud, 1927, p. 38) may have different bounds with reality. I present here four possibilities.

(1) There will be a portion working within the area of the anxiety as signal, able to produce a sort of "tentative motion" inside the preconscious structure by quantum circulation through its preconscious system, just before deciding on a discharge into the outer world. During this phase, previous to discharge, signal anxiety will lead the course of association inside the representational labyrinth of the preconscious system. Later on, after this preconscious thought, the ego gives the order of specific motion.

When dealing with non-interdicted drives (which are the majority in ordinary life), the ego uses repression to serve sublimation. Thus, in the same way as a mental functioning, the cannibalistic oral function gets to "chew up" concepts, the anal function to "evacuate" useless material (expulsive anal function) and to "retain" useful concepts (retentive anal function). Phallic synthesis leads to specific action. These ideas were particularly well developed in our circles by David Liberman (Liberman, 1970; Liberman y Maldavsky, 1975). They are included within the function of realistic anxiety.

When the pleasure principle is conditioned to the reality principle, the signal of anxiety is used by the ego to protect itself from dangers coming from the outside world (realistic anxiety). We understand that the Nirvana principle is conditioned to the pleasure principle (Freud, 1938b). In this way, when the ego complies with its synthetic function, not only does it meet structural harmony among the id, the superego and the outside world, but also reconciles the three principles of instinctual economy: Nirvana, pleasure, reality. Therefore, we can give the name of "normal portions" to this portion of the ego.

(2) Other areas of the ego solve, in an economical way, the circulation of the charges following the neurotic model. They do so through inhibitions and symptoms—signal anxiety—destined to avoid automatic anxiety (Freud, 1926a). The libido introverts and charges memories that obtain their charge from sexual phantasies out of which the neurotic symptom is originated.

(3) Some other areas of the ego will do a "psychotic" reading of reality and consequently will dispose of instinctual solutions. Quantum will push its way out as if there is no frustration limiting desire (Bion, 1967). It will construct a new reality in which "no"

does not exist (Freud, 1923a). Admitting the "no" would mean a narcissistic breakdown of the entire ego (terror) (Lutenberg, 1995a).

(4) Following Bleger's ideas, we can conceive that there exists a syncretic portion of the personality. This portion generates symbiotic bindings that eternize and paralyse evolution. Within the syncretic link, different parts of the "ego", the "superego" and the "id" of the participants remain united. This gives rise to a complementary and supplementary, indiscriminate functioning.

Mental void is a virtual state of the psyche which becomes evident only when these symbiotic bindings get dismantled or broken. The existence of a symbiotic link witnesses early traumatic situations. Sometimes they correspond to trans-generational mourning instances of very traumatic migrations (Lutenberg, 1994, 1995b). Secondary symbiosis itself is a defence against void and terror. It renders the bound syncretic portion eternal, generating aspects of personality which remain apart from evolution. When people, who are participants of symbiotic links, suffer object losses, they always undergo substitutions and practically never go through mourning processes. Once they have reached the corresponding object substitution, they get symbiotically fused to the replacing object, achieving, in this way, an equilibrium of their emotional stability. If this process fails, the result will be a mental vacuum.

The baby is born with an "id" full of different proto-phantasies and a genetic disposition to be developed. The presence of another human being is indispensable for this development to occur. It is a long process that is adequately carried on only if there exists a total fusion with the mother during the first periods of the baby's mental evolution. Such fusion occurs in a natural way through the primal symbiotic link. This link involves the mind and body of both, mother and baby, at the same time.

To Winnicott (Winnicott, 1982), terror appears due to very early, repetitive, void experiences, and the fear of facing them in the future. He conceives a primal stage of indifferentiation that develops because of the possibilities offered by the facilitating environment. This facilitating environment provides "holding", "handling" and "presentation of the object". To Winnicott, the idea of void is related to his conception of the evolution of the psychical apparatus. It belongs to primal stages of "non-integration" that he specifically differentiates from "disintegration".

Bion's theory also helped me to conceptualize mental void. Bion (1965, 1967, 1970) describes a particular apparatus of thoughts. Its key to generate thoughts is constituted by the mother through the reverie function, and also by the baby's whole genetic potential for development. It is on the basis of these two elements that the baby can develop the alpha-function. Such a function produces alpha-elements, suitable for thinking thoughts. When this function is absent, beta-elements are produced, which are only suitable for massive projective identifications.

The problem that these massive projective identifications produce is that when the patient tries to think a thought, this actually gives way to "mental voiding". This is overcome when beta-elements are expelled. All this is due to the fact that the expelled beta-elements host the intolerable emotions to be eliminated, the capacity for registration, belonging to those emotions, as well as the mental capacity for thinking them. By expelling all these components into the external world, the mind undergoes a plundering and emptying process.

The violence of the massive projective identification may eject its components out into infinite space or may eliminate its contents into an object in the external space. In the latter case, a "bizarre object" is formed and this bizarre object replaces an absence (frustration). The objects of the sexual life of these patients, as well as the image of the analyst himself, undertake, very often, the characteristic of a bizarre object.

This theoretical distinction has many clinical implications, since the bizarre object condenses the primal qualities of the object. To these, there is the addition of multiple "functions" attached to the object, which are derived from the psychotic aspect of the patient, through massive projective identification. The bizarre object has its own motility and vitality derived from the projection of the subject and stands for the thought, born after admitting "absence" or frustration.

Frustration imposes on thinking a task, the clue of which is given by the functions of the mind as continent. It is quite different to analyse mental contents (phantasies, memories and own resistances) from the fact of analysing the failures of the mind as continent.

In general, patients suffering mental void do not register

frustration because the defensive symbiotic fusion avoids it through their sexual activity. What is distinctive of these sexual experiences is that their primal aim is not sexual satisfaction, but the achievement of a fusional link, split off from the individual's whole social life, as well as from the rest of his personality. Andrew mentioned this in an explicit way: after the fusional experience during sexual intercourse, his sexual object (and his dependent aspects placed in it) should disappear ... and then renew the circuit.

Very often, sexual experiences carried out in order to shape an exaggerated masculine identity, followed by polymorphous sexual behaviour of different kinds, are attempts at evolution, an evolution that has probably been somehow interrupted during their lives. Not always should we attribute all sexual disturbances to perversion. This may refer to sexual experiences through which certain aspects of personality may develop, namely those aspects linked with mental void, hidden behind invisible symbiotic bindings.

CHAPTER FIVE

Offending gender—being and wanting in male same-sex desire[1]

Martin Stephen Frommer

T he hegemony of gender in theorizing sexuality has made sexual orientation the principal organizer of erotic experience. This has resulted in a heterosexual–homosexual binary in which male heterosexuality is presumed to hinge on the eroticization of difference, while male homosexuality has been understood as a desire for likeness. In this essay, I argue that this view of male same-sex desire is forced by the dominant heterosexist discourse that splits being and wanting into mutually exclusive categories for its understanding of normative heterosexual desire. Examining the psychic consequences of this forced splitting in both straight and gay men, I argue that subjective experiences of difference are no less central to same-sex desire and that, in gay and straight contexts alike, defensive forms of complementarity often wreak havoc with the capacity to love.

Intellect, in its effort to explain (desire), got stuck in the mud like an ass. [Rumi, 1207–1273; Persian]

[I]n love, there is a sort of antipathy, or opposing passion. Each strives to be the other, and both together make up one whole. [Samuel Taylor Coleridge, 1772–1824; English]

Before I can begin talking about desire between men, I need to give voice to a dilemma. I find myself with intentions that are at cross-purposes. On one hand, I seek to further a psychoanalytic understanding of the category of persons who identify as gay and to compare and contrast their relational experience to men who identify as straight. On the other hand, I want to advance a postmodern perspective regarding gender and sexuality which challenges the heterosexual–homosexual binary and the resulting discourse that has been used to define two different kinds of men: those who are straight and those who are gay. In short, I want to contest and disassemble the very category of person I mean to explore.

This conflict has personal ramifications for me. Although I am a man who identifies as gay, a part of me chafes at the label, and while I am certainly not immune to internalized homophobia, I believe this chafing has a different origin. I will try to explain by posing some questions that reflect the ongoing debate between essentialist and constructivist theories as they attempt to make sense of human experience. Does a person's sexuality define his or her identity in any essential way? Is there anything core, unified, or coherent about being gay or straight aside from the particular cultural oppression or privilege associated with each identity category? Who is a gay man? What constitutes this category of personhood?

The problem is this: identity categories impose commonality and coherence by ignoring the actual diversity and ambiguity of lived experience. For example, many men who engage in sex with other men consider themselves neither homosexual nor bisexual, because their sexual role in same-sex experience, as inserter during intercourse or oral sex, preserves what is culturally consistent with heterosexual male behaviour. In contrast, a supervisee of mine treats a man who is married to a woman and has never had sex with another male, yet thinks of himself as gay because of his homoerotic fantasy life and his feelings of identification with gay men. I know men who identify as queer, not gay, and with this self-designation emphasize and celebrate their own non-normativity in gender and sexual practice, where object choice along gender lines fails to capture the essence of what propels their desire. These examples challenge the conceptual integrity of the gay–straight binary, which like all identity binaries, creates and sustains a social order by reducing heterogeneity to homogeneity.

To proceed, I must acknowledge the unresolvable tension between my desire to contest and disassemble the category of "gay man" and my need to maintain it as a category of lived experience—a "false truth" (Goldner, 1991), if you will. Categories of sexuality may be ultimately social constructs; these categories, however, constitute psychic reality (Butler, 1998; Layton, 1998). For gay men, this paradox creates a unique and powerful dilemma: they must be able to negotiate a "good enough" sense of themselves as men, while simultaneously giving expression to erotic desire that is inconsistent with, if not in violation of, culturally normative masculinity.

The gendering of desire

It's three o'clock in the morning, and I'm having difficulty sleeping. I turn on the TV and start channel surfing. I pause, finding myself more awake when I come upon the image of a young, athletic-looking male with muscular chest and arms. Wearing only shorts, socks, and sneakers, he is demonstrating the use of home exercise equipment. I've been hooked by an infomercial. As I watch Randy work out (the announcer by this time has introduced us to him), I hear the voice-over say, as part of his pitch, "Randy's got the body all you guys want!" Hmmm. Randy's got the body all you guys want. I wonder for a moment if I'm watching a gay cable channel but quickly realize that the double entendre reflects my own subjectivity. Randy's body is appealing to me—it's the body I'd like to have—in two ways: as the body I'd like my body to look like—the way I'd like to be—but also, as the body I lust for, the object of my desire. In other words, I identify with and desire the same object.

In contrast, consider how heterosexuality has been understood both culturally and psychodynamically as the eroticization of difference, of opposition. Normative sexuality constitutes a polarity between being and wanting—between identification and desire. In most psychoanalytic theory (Freud, 1923, pp. 28–39, 1924a, pp. 73–79; Klein, 1932; Fairbairn, 1944; Kernberg, 1980; Chasseguet-Smirgel, 1985), this split between identification and desire is maintained. Take for example, the following statement by Ethel

Person (as summarized by Chodorow, 1992), which illustrates the way in which identification and desire are constructed in traditional accounts of psychosexual development:

> In the "normal" course of development, the child consolidates her or his identification with the same gender parent and *this identification enables and fuels desire for the opposite sex*. Gender identification here leads to opposite sex object choice, as a complementary relationship replaces an identificatory relationship ... in the normal course of development, the yearning that attaches to idealization is transformed from the wish to be like to the wish to be with. Desire shifts toward complementariness. [Chodorow, 1992, p. 287, my italics]

This account ties gender identification to object choice in a powerfully prescriptive fashion. Person describes a stable, fixed structure of identification and a stable, fixed structure of desire, in a relationship of opposites, a "complementarity", that is privileged over the desire for likeness. Psychosexual maturity is thus determined by a shift from the wish to be *like* (identificatory love, see Benjamin, 1988) to the erotization of difference and opposition. The implication is that to identify with and desire the same person is abnormal or immature.

What is the fate of same-sex desire when it rubs up against hetero/normative discourse, with its fundamental splitting between identification and desire? How to explain homosexual love without disturbing the bedrock assumptions of the heterosexual imperative?

Typically, psychoanalytic thinking has solved the problem of male same-sex desire within the framework of oedipal discourse. In one variant, gay men are said to be female identified; psychically, they want what women want (Freud, 1910b, pp. 63–117; Blos, 1962; Tyson & Tyson, 1990). This paradigm preserves the polarity between identification and desire. Such a theoretical strategy is culturally supported by a powerful cultural stereotype. For example, a sophisticated woman in her early fifties is talking with me about a former boyfriend. When I ask why the relationship ended, she explains that he had "gender difficulties". When I remain confused, she says, with some irritation at my not getting it, "He turned out to be gay." Her understanding of her boyfriend's sexuality falls back on gender to explain sexual desire. If one is a man and desires a man, one must really be like a woman. In a second strategy, gay men are seen not so much as *like* women, but rather as lacking a firm masculine identification and thus desiring other men in an effort to bolster their own flagging masculinity or incorporate a more adequate sense of themselves as men (Nunberg, 1938; Bibring, 1940; Socarides, 1968; Friedman, 1988). Within this perspective, gay male desire is seen as a desire for likeness, a view that is central to the characterization of homosexual object choice as inherently narcissistic.

Thus, in both culture and psychoanalysis, heterosexuality is construed as the eroticization of difference, and homosexuality the eroticization of likeness. What is obvious but insufficiently theorized, however, is this: the difference that makes all the difference—the difference that is privileged—is genital difference. And the only likeness that counts is genital likeness. As Chodorow (1992) points out, defining sameness and difference merely in terms of genital anatomy collapses the complexity of any individual's sexual object choice.

Consider the following example from a recent session in which a straight male patient is describing his having fallen in love with a woman he recently met. "She's my soul mate," he says. "She's so like me, and I'm so like her; we finish each other's sentences; we know what each other is thinking; we were cut from the same cloth. I see myself in her. I've never felt so like another human being before." This man waxes rhapsodic about the feeling of identificatory love with his partner. (While some might propose that the thrill of this experience of identification is that it emerges in the context of difference, the patient has not framed it that way.) Consider now another example: a gay male patient speaks with desire for his lover: "His body is lanky and smooth. I love it when he cuddles up into my broader, hairy chest. He's softer than I am, both in body and soul. And that's good for me; it softens me too." Here it is the experience of difference that is salient in this man—difference that is valued. (We might characterize this as "difference" in the context of "sameness", but, once again, the man is not pointing to sameness—we are.)

Knowing the nominal gender of two sexual partners thus provides no presumptive understanding of which subjective experience—likeness or difference—characterizes the experience of desire within the dyad. Moreover, the experience of the other and of oneself in relation to the other changes, often reflecting complex combinations of similarity and difference, but certainly not limited to gender (Harris, 1991). I want to rethink this dichotomy between identification and desire in understanding both homosexuality and heterosexuality. The relationship between being and wanting is much less conceptually tidy than oedipal theory would suggest. This untidiness is revealed in the subjectivity of women and men, both straight and gay. Consider, for example, the ruminations of the female protagonist in *Ordinary Love*, a novel by Jane Smiley (as cited in Hansell, 1998): "Now that I can hardly remember what he looked like or what his bed was like, I'm sure that what I really wanted was not to love him but to be him" (p. 347). Along similar lines, Wayne Koestenbaum, in *The Queen's Throat*, a book about opera, homosexuality, and desire, recalls:

> spending much of [my] childhood trying to distinguish identification from desire, asking myself, "Am I in love with Julie Andrews, or do I think I am Julie Andrews?" I knew that to love Julie Andrews placed me, however vaguely, in heterosexuality's domain; but to identify with Julie Andrews ... to want to be the Star of Stars, placed me under suspicion. [p. 18]

Although men are forbidden to identify consciously with women or with femininity, I think it is relevant to ponder the concurrent fascination that exists in our culture with men impersonating or being transformed into women, as in contemporary movies such as *Tootsie*, *Mrs Doubtfire*, *Orlando*, and *The Crying Game*. This fascination with drag, I believe, speaks to the unconscious identifications heterosexual men experience with women, identifications that seek some form of representation and expression, no matter how disguised or displaced.

These examples quarrel with psychoanalytic theories that stress the polarity and independence of identification and desire in favour of a more varied, dynamic, anxious tension between desire and identification, each of which influences, gives form to, and even threatens to fold into the other. Take, for example, Borch-Jacobsen's (1988) proposition that the very act of desiring always involves the unconscious desire to be the subject one desires. From this perspective, desire is fuelled by unconscious identifications with the object one desires. Conversely, Butler (1995) suggests that the very act of identifying with the other—of claiming likeness with the other—may be the consequence of an already existing, but repudiated desire for the other, which lives on as an identification. We may consciously give up what we must not desire (i.e. boys if we are boys, girls if we are girls), but they remain as unconscious wishes.

Recently, Hansell (1998), in an attempt to elucidate the psychodynamics of heterosexuality, has taken Butler's (1995) premise and added developmental content. In his account of male heterosexual development, he argues that, for boys who will become heterosexually oriented, homosexuality is only gradually renounced and then primarily as a non-masculine trait, as part of an ongoing process of self-as-male differentiation, which requires that the boy disown any identifications with femininity.

Building on the early work of Chodorow (1978), Hansell (1998) speaks of the early pressures to renounce gender-inconsistent traits as being more intense for boys than for girls. Boys must simultaneously negotiate separation and gender differentiation from their mothers, whereas girls normally remain gender identified with their mothers while they negotiate separation from them. In the developmental story Hansell constructs to explain male heterosexuality, he stresses that boys negotiate the strongest pressure to renounce homosexual feelings and feminine identifications at a time in their development when their egos are immature. In Piagetian terms, this is the same period when their cognitive processes are preoperational, when they are still perceptually bound, with thinking that is predominantly "all or nothing" and largely concrete. These constraints result in greater rigidity of gender solutions for boys, where masculinity and femininity, first encountered through a lens of an either/or trade-off, are seen as mutually exclusive ways of being. Thus, male heterosexuality can be thought to rest uneasily on the requirement for some sort of reassurance from an underlying gender anxiety, a reassurance that comes by way of reiterating the mantra of sexual difference. The split is defensive, with the goal of denying the anxiety-laden dynamic tension, instability, and permeability of the boundaries between identification and desire. In heterosexual love, the creation of this rigid, defensive complementarity combines with sexism, such

that the desiring male subject must define the woman as an inferior
other in order to desire "femininity" (Hansell, 1998).

Analogously, the cultural creation of the gay man as "faggot"
functions as a container for the denigrated, disclaimed aspects of the
straight man's same-sex desire. He needs the woman to hold his
femininity, and he needs the gay man to hold his homosexual
desire. These projective processes are implicated in common gender
pathologies. In men, they often lead to the splitting of sex and
dependency, thereby gaining the safety of a power advantage—
male dominance, if you will. The analogous response in women is to
eroticize domination, such that submission ensures the experience
of being desired. These defensive structures, says Chodorow (1992),
become normalized in cultural life and are reproduced in the minds
of children who grow up internalizing these modes of relating.

I will make use of this account of heterosexuality to further our
discussion about sameness and difference in erotic desire. Butler
and Hansell (1998) conceive of male heterosexuality as resting on a
defensive use of a complementarity organized around the gender
binary. The experience of difference is unconsciously appropriated
by the male subject in an attempt to block from consciousness a
fluidity of fantasy that may include feared identifications with the
female object of desire. Actually, the excitement in heterosexual
desire may stem from the very wish to jump the fence, to feed for a
moment in the forbidden pastures of likeness, before retreating once
again to the safety of difference. The desire that we term as
homosexual may permit more pleasure in likeness, since in same-
sex desire there appears to be a more conscious recognition of the
potential to identify with and desire the same object.

But this schematic contrast is more apparent than real. In male
homosexual desire, the tension between masculinity and femininity
does not vanish, as a dynamic force, simply because the nominal
gender of both subjects is masculine. Gay men are socialized like
straight men in that masculinity requires contending with the
"problem" of femininity. To paraphrase Butler (1998), "If one is a
man ... then wanting a man will bring being a man into question ...
'(B)eing a man' or 'being a woman' has everything to do with
finding a right direction for desire; one that confirms both gender
identity and sexuality" (p. 375).

Thus, men who desire men often make use of defensive forms of complementarity just as men who desire women do. Defensive uses of complementarity or difference do not differentiate heterosexual from homosexual love. Indeed, they serve a similar defensive function: to quell the anxiety that emanates from the fact that masculinity, for all men, is a tenuous psychological business. For men, gay and straight, the pursuit of sexual desire is fraught with the potential for narcissistic vulnerability along gender lines, although the subjective experience of sameness and difference, in relation to the object of desire, is often enlisted to regulate such feelings.

For men who desire men, for example, sharing the same gender class with the object of their desire can create a heightened potential for vulnerability. When a man desires another man and experiences rejection by him, that rejection is not only felt to be a rejection of himself as a love object; it can also be experienced as a rejection of himself as a "like subject". As one man put it, "I can't get myself to approach another man in a bar when it's obvious I'm interested in him, because there's too much of myself at stake: if he rejects me, it not only feels that he's unattracted to me, it feels like he's saying, 'You don't measure up as a man. You're not a member of the club.' " Men, with women, also experience vulnerability along gender lines when they suffer rejection, but there is a built-in safety net to cushion the fall; reasserting the discourse of difference is often the route taken to soothe such wounds. "What else could I expect," says one man to another. "She's a woman—you know how they are."

Psychoanalytic theorizing about male homosexuality has it backwards. The basic thesis has been that narcissistic difficulties in gay men cause a desire for likeness. In fact, however, subjective experiences of difference are also central to same-sex desire. Moreover, narcissistic vulnerability along gender lines does not *produce* same sex desire, but it is almost always a *product of* it.

Clinical material

Stuart entered treatment because of the huge disparity he experienced between his professional and his personal life. A high-level executive in a multinational corporation, he had achieved by his mid-forties extraordinary success in the business world, success he had accomplished as an "out" gay man. He reported his business success as having been due, in no small measure, to his being able to intuit and meet every need of the CEO. Stuart's life was active both professionally and socially. He would often work long hours flying around the world, then travel on weekends to gay resorts and attend all the right circuit parties. But his personal life ultimately felt lonely and unfulfilled. In fantasy he longed for what he had never experienced—a close, intimate, sexual relationship with another man.

His actual sexual and emotional life with men left much to be desired. He found himself attracted exclusively to young men, usually in their mid-twenties. Together, we came to dub these men "lost boys". They were often from less privileged backgrounds and troubled families, with little direction in life, and he took them under his wing, working hard to win their favour, and nurturing them, both emotionally and financially. While these men offered him companionship for a time, sooner or later he wound up feeling disappointed in the quality of these relationships. His own needs often went unmet, and eventually he wound up feeling duped: they would stay out all night partying, have sex with other men, or become less available to him sexually. Things usually ended in a mess. In between these relationships, or when they were headed for the rocks, Stuart would hire hustlers through an escort service. This he strongly preferred to cruising and the hit-or-miss of trying to pick men up. He spoke frankly about the pleasure he derived from these encounters. He was able to totally objectify hustlers—they were in his service and he found great relief in not having to meet their needs or worry about their feelings, as he did with the young men with whom he became involved. With hustlers, he never felt self-conscious about his penis size or restricted in asking for what he wanted sexually, which was often to be the passive partner in anal intercourse. "If he thinks I'm a poor specimen of a man, so what? He's there to serve me. I'm paying him. He can't hurt me," he would say. Stuart admired men who were able to go into bars and go after what they wanted. When he thought about doing that, he found himself with thoughts and feelings he recalled from the fifth grade: he was attracted to boys in his class, ashamed and worried that they would find out, and frightened of feeling humiliated. The men he might want to approach in a bar had the capacity to make him feel awful about himself as a man, the way those kids might have and also the way his father did, when he voiced dissatisfaction with Stuart's appearance.

Stuart describes himself as a late-maturing, scrawny boy. "I'd watch my father looking at other boys. 'Why don't you slick your hair back like so and so?' he'd say. It boggled my mind. He didn't realize I had curly hair, and it just wasn't possible. He didn't want to see me the way I was."

In sessions with me, Stuart aimed to please. In many ways, he behaved like an ideal patient. He was invested in his therapy and made it clear that he often scheduled important meetings around our sessions. Although he was prone to a form of discourse that I imagine resembled his father's—very detailed, somewhat pedantic, and devoid of emotion—I clearly felt his desire to communicate his experience to me, and I seldom felt bored. In response to questions I posed to him regarding his feelings toward me, he would often tell me how good he thought I was in my work and how much respect he had for me. And just in case I was wondering, he also let me know he had no interest whatsoever in me sexually, which in certain ways saddened him, since he saw me as a more appropriate partner for him than the men who, in fact, did interest him. He wished he could feel attraction for someone he experienced to be more like himself.

As the treatment progressed, Stuart would grow anxious when he found himself with little to say, especially when I did not fill in the silences for him. He would worry about our not connecting; he felt he was not doing his part right. Over time he became able to describe his associations at these moments; these often included his father, sitting in an easy chair, his face covered by a newspaper. He was absorbed in his reading and unavailable: "How do I get his attention? How do I engage him? I knew what it felt like to be with him when he was delighted with me, but at these times I knew that if I interrupted him he'd be irritated, so I'd just sit and wait."

During periods of silence between us, Stuart worried that I felt distracted and that my attention would wander. "It's not clear with you," he'd say. "But when I know for sure that you're engaged, I feel better." This anxiety about connections and about losing them became a theme we elaborated over time. It often seemed to come down to the following: unless Stuart experienced himself as performing—showing his prowess—he worried that men would have no need for him. His just being there was not enough to make someone want to connect with him.

During the course of treatment, as Stuart became more able to formulate his emotional experience in relation to different men in his life, he became more aware of how his anxiety about himself was organized along gender lines and how his choices of young men and hustlers helped him to defend against a particular form of gender anxiety. "My feelings about myself as a man shift, depending on where I am and who I'm with. I don't walk around feeling faggy or effeminate all the time. It only becomes an issue at certain times, like when my sexual attractiveness is on the line, like when I walk into a bar and find myself cruising. Earlier in the day, at a business meeting, I felt strong, powerful and very masculine in the way I handled myself. I wish I could feel that way when I'm going out to meet men." Associating with men in their twenties, Stuart felt secure in a role similar to his father's, with more knowledge and experience, and therefore more prowess. Since with these men he most often played the role of the top sexually, he maintained a sense of himself that was protected from feelings of humiliation. Stuart's ability to objectify hustlers allowed him to fend off anxiety and humiliation. He could ask for what he wanted sexually without fearing that he would be thought of as "a little girl".

During the first years of our work together, Stuart kept me very much on a pedestal. He claimed that he never thought about me outside of his experience of me in the office. He knew I was gay from the get-go, since he had deliberately sought out a referral to a gay-identified therapist. However, he was very wary of finding out more about me, partly because he worried that either he would learn things that would disappoint him or that differences he would discover between us could possibly disrupt our bond. As time has gone on, I have deliberately chosen to share aspects of my own emotional responses to him. I have let him know when I feel cut off from him in sessions and when I feel moved by what he is saying. Recently, traces of flirtatiousness and exchanges shaded with the glimmer of erotic possibility have emerged between us. For most of the treatment, while I have been very aware of a fondness for him, sexual feelings have been absent from my own subjectivity. Now I am aware of finding him more physically appealing and can even imagine having sex with him. I think this recent shift in my feelings toward him parallels a comparable shift inside him; he too feels more of a sense of emotional possibility between us, although I doubt he would acknowledge the erotic elements. However, he seems less frightened of me and is more aware of his thoughts and feelings about me.

Most recently, he has begun to speculate about aspects of my personality that might give him difficulty were we to have a different kind of relationship. Not surprisingly, this expanded interest in me parallels his new awareness of finding several men, closer to his own age, sexually attractive, although he remains ambivalent about acting on these feelings. Recently, after meeting a man in his forties at a party, Stuart came to a session excited, almost giddy: "I really liked his masculinity and his maturity—it's amazing to me that I felt turned on. Last night I fantasized about letting him be in the father role, the controlling figure, and about my not having to perform so much, but at the same time I'm very excited and very afraid. I didn't invite him back to the apartment because I wasn't ready to have sex with him. If he's not the kid and he's not a hustler, who am I going to be and what will he think of me?"

Discussion

I understand Stuart's exclusive attraction for a particular genre of young man to reflect a defensive use of complementarity. This trope towards difference serves several defensive functions. By locating the "boy" in the other, he attempts to disavow the boy in himself, who is vulnerable to the mature man's harsh judgment: the father for whom he does not measure up. At another level, Stuart's pursuit of difference in the form of rakish young men may be understood as a desire to take in the adolescent boy with the slicked back hair that both he and his father admired/desired. This was an effort to repair his own defective sense of himself along gender lines, which reached its height during his own adolescence.

Stuart's ability to experience desire and sexual gratification was severely restricted by his need to protect himself from anxiety and shame from men whom he admired and no doubt desired on an unconscious level. He was able to experience sexual gratification with men closer to his age only when he was able to hire them, objectify them, and reduce them to objects of use. In other contexts, with men who were his peers, Stuart led with the more competitive part of himself as a defence against allowing himself to desire them.

The shift in this treatment can be seen as following a trajectory from desire hinged to complementarity to the beginnings of the desire for a "like subject". Stuart's ability to desire men more like himself suggests an increment in his ability to like himself as a man. But I would argue against the linearity of this interpretation. Interpreting the movement as a shift from desiring difference to desiring sameness fails to capture the actual complexity that exists in the multiple layers of psychic experience that coexist and mediate all forms of subjectivity, including desire. It is not, in fact, the case that Stuart's interest in young men has diminished. He continues to be drawn to men from another generation who exude an air of confidence and spunk. His new and fragile interest in men more like himself, coexists with this more prominent and familiar passion.

A more accurate depiction of this state of affairs would be to say that the *range of relational possibilities is expanding*, that he is less restricted in who or what can spark his desire. For example, Stuart's desire for a "like subject" may signal the reawakening of another complementarity in which he is the boy who desires and yearns to be desired by the man (father). This internalized relationship has been filled with apprehension, anxiety, and fear of being found lacking. As he permits himself to feel connected with a father (figure in sex), where he can allow for experiences including feeling smaller, weaker, and passive in relation to the other, there is both the risk of shame and rejection, but also the possibility for deep gratification.

In Stuart's internal world and romantic life, being the father has been a defence against his wish to be fathered and against desiring his father, another variant on Butler's (1995) argument that thwarted desire turns into identification. The rigidity in his sexual life is a consequence of his need to fend off certain threatening and painful psychic experiences. The growth taking place in this treatment is increasing Stuart's tolerance for experiencing multiple complementarities in his psychic life and the affects associated with them. Freedom to desire is an outgrowth of feeling free to experience a multiplicity of simultaneous, alternating, and contra-dictory experiences of sameness and difference.

I have tried to illustrate that the pursuit of difference through defensive complementarity is no less characteristic of same-sex desire than of cross-sex desire. It is simply that *gender* (or, more precisely, genital difference) is not the ultimate pivot on which erotics hinge. Difference may serve both defensive and non-defensive functions. The desire for difference can be about the repudiation of aspects of the self—by locating problematic aspects of the self in the other and relating to the disavowed self in ways that maintain the experience of difference. The pursuit of difference may also reflect the desire to possess, control, or dominate the other as a means of importing into the self what is experienced as absent or deficient. One can be irresistibly drawn to "otherness", as in unfamiliarity, to escape a familiarity that is associated with pain and trauma. Difference may also be about novelty, in which one's relation to the other is not primarily about importing or exporting but, rather, about appreciating difference in the other simply for the sake of difference.

The pull towards likeness is equally complex. It can be about the wish for merger or the need for mirroring. Merger can be a transcendent experience or a defence against the experience of difference and separateness in both homosexual and heterosexual arrangements. Rigid, defensive patterns of complementarity, where the recognition of likeness is not permitted, as well as rigid patterns of sameness, in which experiences of difference are defended against—the need to maintain difference or sameness at any cost—signal, in both homosexual and heterosexual contexts, significant narcissistic difficulties. The more restricted or rigid the requirements of likeness or difference, the more restricted and conditional is the sexual and emotional gratification that is possible. When deviation from a required pattern or scheme occurs, love is laced with pain and fear. The relevant distinction here is not rigidity versus fluidity, but rigidity versus flexibility. Rigid forms of difference or sameness are often defences against anxiety about instability—the worry that difference may dissolve into sameness or sameness may dissolve into difference. But the desire for sameness does not inherently define narcissistic love, nor does the desire for difference distinguish object love from love that is narcissistic. Loving that is termed narcissistic is not about *whom* one loves, but *how* one loves. It is an error to attempt to articulate a dichotomy between narcissistic loving and loving that is object oriented. It makes more sense to view, as Freud (1914) ultimately did, narcissistic modes of desiring as coexisting with modes of love that are more object oriented, where anxiety and feelings of vulnerability often determine the ebb and flow between the two.

Clinical implications

In a homophobic and heterosexist culture, the experiences of shame and narcissistic vulnerability are *core* to the lives of men who offend gender through their expression of same-sex desire. It is only recently that psychoanalytic theory and practice have begun to appreciate the powerful impact of the social context on the psychic experience of gay men. (For examples of analytic work conducted from this perspective, see Frommer, 1994; Blum & Pfetzing, 1997; and Drescher, 1998.)

Gay men need support in becoming more comfortable with their own non-normative versions of masculinity that incorporate same-sex desire. Our task as analysts is not to maintain the norm, but to broaden the scope of masculinities gay and straight men can wear with a feeling of pride and pluck about themselves. We need to make room for multiple narratives about how boys grow into men—narratives that capture the diversity of human experience—without privileging some stories and stigmatizing others (see Corbett, 1996, for example).

The most productive arena for reworking issues of gender, sexuality, and shame is the ongoing relational life of the psycho-analytic dyad. However, we as therapists must analyse how we have used gender to organize our internal experience and structure our relationships (Goldner, 1991) and how the binaries of gender and sexuality intersect in our particular psyches to form prescriptive relationships between the two.

The analyst's capacity to work with his or her personal response to the patient's homoerotic desire is crucial to treatment outcome. Whether a mutual collusion will occur to avoid the patient's underlying shame, or whether the analyst will find the patient's shaming self and bring it into the relationship, is a central crossroads in the treatment. It is the analyst's subjectivity, often rationalized by commitments to a psychoanalytic theory that reifies the opposition between identification and desire, that determines the course of treatment (see Frommer, 1995).

As analysts, we need actively to question and challenge our patients as well as ourselves when the experience of human attributes becomes cast in our minds as exclusively masculine or exclusively feminine (Layton, 1998). A critical analytic stance can help us to counter the excessive reliance on binary thinking that characterizes so much of human thought and is so pervasive in both cultural and psychoanalytic discourse. We need both to recognize and to keep in mind that categories like masculine–feminine and gay–straight are actually culturally sanctioned instances of splitting (Benjamin, 1988; Dimen, 1991; Goldner, 1991; Layton, 1998). Holding the psychic tension between the knowledge that gender and sexuality are socially constructed and yet lived as psychic realities can create a transitional space in which to experience them (Dimen, 1991).

From this perspective, we can free sexuality from the hegemony of gender. We can begin to conceive of erotic experience as hinging less on the hollow concept of sexual orientation and more on a dynamic interplay of contradictory identifications and complementarities. Simply put, the mystery of desire rests on who we allow ourselves to be and what we allow ourselves to want.

Note

1. This paper, entitled "Offending Gender: Being and Having in Male Same-Sex Desire" was originally published in the journal *Studies in Gender and Sexuality*, Vol 1, pages 191–206 published by Analytic Press.

CHAPTER SIX

The battle of the sexes[1]

Jorge Kantor

T he first thing one can clearly say about the battle of the sexes is that the conflict has not yet finished. Many and varied generations would be necessary (thanks to this mixture of Darwinism and Lamarckism in which human beings evolve), before men and women can achieve a *good enough* equilibrium in order openly to maintain that the long battle of the sexes has finally come to an end.

Freud, in "Civilization and its Discontent", would have said that it is difficult to believe that the human species will be able to reach such a level of satisfaction. But, let us agree, at least, that this new millennium comes with the hope of achieving a better understanding between the loving enemies.

Although it would be *politically correct* to insist on the equivalence between men and women, emphasizing common themes since we are all members of the same species, a psychoanalytical framework is forced to acknowledge the existence of the differences in gender as an essential starting point. In other words, for psychoanalysis, brain and mind possess a sexual identity.

I would like to emphasize that this distinction must take into account the generation factor: one is either *son* or *daughter* before being *mother* or *father*. Gender studies must necessarily include these generation determinants. Antigone and Jocaste, Oedipus and Laius are all archetypal interpreters of psychoanalytical mythology. You, your husband, your wife, your children; or you, your mummy, your daddy, brothers and sisters, are all characters in each personal mythology. Each one of us has been, is and/or could be either Antigone or Jocaste, Oedipus or Laius, and if we assume the Freudian bisexuality, we should admit the second gender characters as our own.

Revolution in the original—global—village

The mental form of these binding factors comes in the last instance, from the revolution inferred in the Freudian genesis "Totem and Taboo" (1913) occurring approximately, a hundred thousand years ago when we lived somewhere we would now judge as being paradise, probably in southern Africa.

Current studies hold that in the primogenital village, in the original global village, our distant and common relatives did not exceed five thousand individuals. Everything seems to indicate that humanity is reduced, then, to a number of people that could fit in a small town, no more.

Freud, following Darwin, asserted that these *proto-humans* changed social structure in which they lived in (very much like today's gorillas or chimpanzees), installing new laws of exogamy and the forbidding of incest. They possibly understood, in the darkness of their brains, that their personal interests were better served by inventing rudimentary regulations in their common relationships, instead of continuing to live the way our nice but limited biped relatives still do.

One mythical day we changed our official structure; one day that may have lasted thousands of years, the village's youngsters dethroned the analogue of the white-haired gorilla. In every corner of the prehistoric town, his own children assassinated the head of each clan. The young women no longer wanted to mate with the leader of their family group, they preferred having affairs with the neighbour's sons. Their brothers also longed for the other group of young women.

It was, no doubt, the beginning of the everlasting battle between despotism and democracy. Brothers and sisters assured themselves a better distribution of power and sex, in the supply and demand of everyday relationships between genders, leading to a series of changes that have lasted until today.

It has been almost a hundred thousand years since we began to create the base elements of our present life, and only one thousand years ago the relationship between men and women throughout the globe were very much like those now characterized by the Taliban. Even in our time, the Islamic fundamentalists are not the only ones to act in this way. And even more, these people are not that far away (probably today this kind of treatment, common to the past millennium, is carried out in this same neighbourhood, or even possibly in this very place).

The point I am trying to make is the following: to think that it is going to take many years, hundreds, who knows, to arrive, worldwide, at a fair and deserved equilibrium, is neither an exaggeration nor an absurdity.

I will continue by mentioning two issues, which are currently under debate, in order to contribute to the general understanding of the relationship between genders.

The omission-of-the-vagina

The first has to do with a matter, which is as old as humanity. In a common family structure, the feminine genitals are unnameable; at least in the way other body parts are named. The issue of the genitalia of a son and daughter has always been a complicated matter. The omission of the vagina is, without doubt, a reference to the vast difficulty faced by parents in dealing with their own children's sexuality.

One can speculate that the long gone fact that our primitive parents were the ones that dethroned the tyrannical father has something to do with this. Even though a more convenient society emerged for the youth of the community, wariness towards potential rebellion must have remained underneath. Finally, the children had been able to conquer the jurisdiction of the inaugural father.

Humanity's history emphasizes that eventually God rescued us from our infidelity and showed us the way in order to be on good terms with Him. For this purpose, He invented, like a sort of obligatory levy, circumcision, the sole purpose of which was to express God's power over His creatures. The Bible tells us that Abraham circumcised himself when he was 99 years old, and only then was he, three days later, able to see God's face and to impregnate Sara a few months later, with Isaac; she was 90 years old.

From an iconoclast's perspective, it can be said that God changed Isaac's life, which Abraham was willing to sacrifice in exchange for a small part of his penis. In any case, Isaac must have understood clearly who was in charge.

It is interesting to note that, just as one cannot look directly at God's face, one is not allowed to name Him. In fact, He does not even have a name: *He-Who-He-Is*. Something similar happens on the other end of our hierarchy: the vagina is not named, nor even directly considered. Daughters have to construct their mental apparatus with mechanisms that force them to suppress a part of their own body.

In the end, it is impossible to avoid talking about the vagina, just as it is inevitable not to mention any other part of the human body. Maybe one does not usually mention kidneys or lungs in parent–child interactions, but are quick to talk about the nose, arms or ears. There may even be the hypothetical case of a family where, for reasons yet to be determined, any mention of the knee or nails is omitted during the early development of the children of the house. This would be considered strange by everyone, but it is much harder to conceive a family where hands or mouths are not mentioned.

Male child genitalia are named (although mostly by using a diminutive) while feminine ones lack a proper name. As a compromising formula, it is a common practice for families to include the vagina as a part of the genital–urethra–anal zone; the word *poto* (bottom) is used as a denomination designated for the whole area. Another local possibility is to call the vagina *thing*. The disadvantages of this everyday automatism are evident. That which is not named is turned, in due time, into a "filicide" of sorts. Girls absorb the message that a part of their bodies, one that carries out a central daily function does not have a name, and if it does, it is called a *thing*, a word used to talk about everything and nothing.

The practice of refraining from naming the vagina may be seen as a greatly summarized version of genuine genital mutilation, even though both belong to the same group.

Every day thousands of girls are at risk of being subjected to genital mutilation, a practice which usually has devastating and, sometimes, mortal consequences. Female genital mutilation consists of the total or partial surgical extirpation of the genitals. The origin of these practices is unknown; it existed before Christianity and Islam, and is not a central part of any of the main religions. It expands beyond ethnic and cultural frontiers.

We should not let any part of this inclination towards despotism filter, through projective identification, depriving our daughters of a part of their individuality. It would correspond to baptizing what is missing and doing what is obviously necessary.

What does a two-year-old girl think, or feel, about her vagina? She knows now, and has known for some time, that she has a body, and every day she gets to know it better. However, among the most important things she will learn, will be the ambivalence her socializing agents introduce about that particular part of her body.

This negation will inevitably become an organizing theme, the centre of the sexual theories of the child, certainly a major factor in the organization of her psychic apparatus. The identifications, with which she will structure her body, will show a mental–soma vaginal representative that has incorporated eclipsed elements of the minds of those who socialize her. In the mentalization–materialization process, it will consist of a representation based on an omission, annulment and subordination.

It can thus be understood why it is so easy for us to accept the idea of Mary's virginity.

Paternal endorsement of the newborn

As a final point I will discuss the father's role in the period known as *primary narcissism*. Naturally, I will assume that such a process does in fact take place. As is well known, a sector of our brotherhood maintains that human beings are born spontaneously willing to relate with their caretakers, in other words, *libido is object seeking* (as happens, incidentally, with every other mammal).

Another part of the order maintains that before that happens, people try to complete themselves through a kind of emotional charge that comes from our environment, although newborns carrying out such a task know nothing yet about the existence of others.

Here, the difference between mother and father seems to be obvious. Mother is indispensable so that the new organism becomes a mental entity. There is no such thing as a baby (alone), Winnicott reminds us. We all notice that father enters the child's life later, and it is argued that his role is usually that of the third person who stops the dual fusion between two people, which at one time seemed one.

But it seems unfair to imply that a man cannot take care of a newborn efficiently and lovingly. This way, the father is left out of being a constitutive part in the first frontier the child will be able to recognize, or in other words, he is banned from contributing directly to the *primary narcissism* of his descendants.

However, evolution has favoured a significant peculiarity among humans. It has been observed that a great majority of newborns show, for a number of weeks, some clear characteristics that relate him/her, without any hesitation, to his/her own father: shape of the face, colour of the eyes, etc. Evolution has assured this beginning that accompanies the new family member, and which signals with certainty the child's genetic linkages, guaranteeing the identity that lineage will provide. This help from biology is very well received, since the dictum is fierce: *madre cierta, padre incierto* (certain mother, uncertain father).

To consider that the relationship between a father and his children must only gain importance, at best, during the second year of life, is an anachronistic resignation and a servile error. It is necessary to break the heavy chain we have inherited through many generations. The benefits can only be mutual. The masculine generic tendency must continue directing itself to an increase of contact and participation in the early care of children, learning and getting close to them, without fearing neurotic guilt, borderline envies, nor psychotic streaks.

This is a moment in the evolutionary history of the species in which, I believe, a *breakpoint* has been reached. The conditions are being set for fathers to take an active part in the mothering of the children, if only because we now clearly know that small children need a great amount of affection. It seems that this is the best way in which *object relations* can construct themselves with a lower emotional cost, or in other words, with enough emotional capital to affront emotional expenditures.

It is necessary for men and women, mothers and fathers, to look at themselves more like a combined pair than like an organization of uncommunicative consecutive functions. No one can any longer assert that mothers have nothing to contribute during her children's late socializing, so let us stop thinking that fathers are naturally obtuse and useless with little children.

In short, it may take many a year, possibly hundreds or thousands of years. Each generation tries to follow Darwin's dictum and produce *modified descendants*. For our children to be more able as parents performing this complicated task, is certainly much more difficult than to *teach, govern* or *psychoanalyse*.

Note

1. This paper was presented in a panel at the conference "Al fin de la batalla", held in Lima in November 2001.

CHAPTER SEVEN

The loneliness of the homosexual

Juan-David Nasio

T he reasons why people consult a psychoanalyst are not as wide-ranging as one might think. Basically, they relate to the typical themes of all human life: sexual problems, family conflicts, and issues involving work-place relationships. In terms of the symptoms we are asked to deal with, I would say the phobic patient's fears, the depressed patient's despondency, the hysteric's passionate and tormented lifestyle, and, last but not least, the sheer torture that the obsessional patient's thoughts create.

As to the feeling of unease in contemporary society, I would say without a shadow of a doubt that the main predicament is the problematic question of masculine self-identity. It is quite obvious that the principal dilemma—and the situation is likely to become worse—lies in the steady loss of reference marks that define manliness. This is one of the most distressing dilemmas that I encounter almost on a daily basis in my clinical work: many patients seek help for sexual impotence, premature ejaculation or, more generally, because they find it more and more difficult to know what it means to be a man in a love relationship, a father in the family, or a manager in the work-place.

Paternal authority began to decline in the 1970s. Recent

advances in biotechnology make procreation possible without any recourse to the male at all, and, at the same time, even the father's name is no longer passed on automatically to his offspring. All this means that, in a very distressing way, men feel more and more insecure as to their masculine identity. There is no longer any clear social model with which to identify in order to assert their membership of the masculine community. Traditionally, in patriarchal societies, men represented authority and combativity, while women personified the home, the mother's presence and the wife's supportive role as partner. When women quite properly obtained professional and financial independence, that pattern was irrevocably turned upside down, so that the whole organization of society has had—and still has—to be thought through afresh. Though most people would now accept that these changes are here to stay, we have as yet no clear idea of what the consequences of this situation will be. In the 2090s, for example, what form will the relationship between men and women take? For the moment, it's a mystery! It is fascinating to try to imagine the, as yet unknown, links that a man and a woman will invent in order to love each other.

We can at least be sure of two things today—and my own experience confirms this: firstly, that masculine identity is being profoundly reshaped, and, secondly, that a new form of social attitude with respect to sexuality is developing. For example, when I began practising as a psychoanalyst, homosexuals would seek my help in order to stop being homosexual. I will never forget the first patient I had who lay down on the couch—a woman who was extremely distressed because of her lesbianism. I was about twenty-two years of age at the time, but I already knew that there was absolutely no way in which a homosexual could be changed into a heterosexual. A clearly-defined sexual orientation cannot be altered. Nowadays, homosexual patients do not consult in order to "be cured of their tendencies", but for quite different reasons.

The gay community has succeeded in gaining recognition as such, and it plays a not insignificant role in the fabric of modern society; this was particularly the case in the fight against AIDS, for example. In quite a short time—some twenty years of campaigning—the homosexual movement has acquired rights that would have been inconceivable before 1980. Homophobia is still active, of course, but it is incomparably less virulent than it was just a few years ago. There is no doubt that the social representation of homosexuality has changed radically.

Homosexuality is no longer thought of as a perversion or an illness, as used to be the case; it is a form of love in its own right, a particular way of loving and of feeling loved. Homosexuals seek help because they suffer from a disorder, and a very distressing one at that: loneliness. Some time ago now, a young man called Roger consulted me. He was a very well-educated person, and he held a senior post in the civil service. He said: "Doctor, I'm homosexual. My parents don't know, my brother is the only person I have let into the secret. I'm unhappy because I feel desperately lonely. I don't seem to be able to live in a stable relationship with anyone". *That* is the tragedy of homosexuals in today's society: their emotional solitude. Though they may be socially integrated, deep down they feel terribly isolated. The problem is not so much how to assert their sexual identity as to obtain the love for which every human being craves. If a homosexual wants to satisfy a purely sexual need, he can do so at any time; all he has to do is to go to one of the well-known meeting-places—saunas, public toilets, certain parks or cinemas—and he will soon find a partner for a furtive masturbatory orgasm. But what he *does* miss—and it hurts like an open wound—is affection, tenderness, tying his fate to that of a partner with whom he is in love, brushing his teeth in the same bathroom, going shopping together, travelling together ... in other words, the little things of everyday life. The painful contrast between a high degree of sexual activity and the precarious nature of feelings of love no doubt explains why young gay men find it difficult to set up a stable relationship with one partner. It is only once they reach a certain age that homosexual men settle down in a lasting relationship based on mutual communication and shared projects.

If we confine ourselves to the context of male homosexuality—the world of lesbian women is quite different—it may be worth emphasizing the fact that all men, without exception, have homosexual tendencies and that the homosexual experiments that are so widespread in the immediate post-pubertal period are a perfectly normal phenomenon. It is only when these tendencies harden into a significant sexual preference that we are justified in using the term homosexuality.

To start with, it should be remembered that we are all bisexual!

Bisexuality is a constituent feature of all human beings, both physically and mentally speaking. But this basic form of bisexuality should not be confused with actual bisexual intercourse. It is one thing to assert that each of us has both a masculine and a feminine part in his or her make-up; it is quite another to have actual sexual relations indiscriminately with partners of both sexes. In my experience, clinically speaking, bisexual activity is not a reflection of natural bisexuality at all; it is much more a manifestation of homosexuality. I would go as far as to say that a man who has sexual relations indiscriminately with both male and female partners is basically homosexual; by that I mean that his most deeply-rooted drives will obtain satisfaction only through the carnal contact with the body of another man.

Jacques, another of my patients, had a passionate homosexual relationship as a young man, then married the woman he loved and went on to become a happy father. However, quite unexpectedly, after fifteen years of apparently tranquil heterosexuality, he left his family in order to satisfy his irresistible desire to live with a male friend. In the end, his homosexual drives proved stronger than his bisexual eclecticism.

I said that homosexuality is neither a vice not a perversion, nor can it be called an illness. As far as we psychoanalysts are concerned, homosexuals are, above all, fundamentally narcissistic; in other words, they have an intense attachment to their own body, to their image and to the male sex organ—both their own and that of their partners. It would, however, be a mistake to see in this form of egocentricity a kind of serene and complacent self-love. On the contrary: the homosexual's narcissism is extremely painful. It is a cruel and exaggerated kind of narcissism that makes him feel fragile and over-emotional: at times he feels so sure of himself that he becomes arrogant and uncompromising, at others he belittles himself so much that he is plunged into the depths of despair and loneliness.

That said, how is male homosexuality to be explained? Psycho-analysis considers homosexuality to be a variant of sexual identity brought about by arrested development of the libido, which in turn is caused by an excess of tenderness and desire in the mother that ends up by submerging her son. A mother's excessive tenderness towards her son—often facilitated by the father's absence—locks the, as yet immature, child into an overwhelming sense of pleasure from which he cannot break free. There can be no doubt that some kinds of tenderness are stifling; the one to which the future homosexual was subjected to as a boy is a clear example. Later, when he becomes a young man, strongly influenced by the pleasure he experienced as a boy, he will have a pressing need to seek out the same voluptuousness and the same feelings of happiness. The quest for sensuous pleasure is so omnipresent that it shapes his body and imposes on him a certain way of loving.

The crucial point here is that the homosexual's sybaritism, tastes, and emotional preferences are dictated by an imaginary scene that is permanently at work inside him, often without his noticing it. It is not a clearly-defined picture but a blurred, out-of-focus and unconscious image that includes two characters—the homosexual himself as a child, and his mother, with her arms around him in a sensual embrace. Though this incestuous fantasy is unconscious, it determines the young man's sexual orientation. I can well understand that this sounds astonishing: a fantasy representation imprinted during childhood and of which there is no conscious knowledge is played out involuntarily in the theatre of his love life!

In this imaginary scene, the mother plays the part of the seductress, and the boy is irresistibly attracted to her. Sometimes, without realizing it, a homosexual will actually project this fantasy into his real-life relationship with his partner. He plays—and has his partner play—one or other of the two principal characters, mother and son. If he himself plays the part of the seductress, he attributes to his partner that of the child seduced—and *vice versa*. Acting the fantasy of incestuous seduction in this way explains why a homosexual may try to find a partner that resembles the child he once was. Consequently, through his love for this man, the homosexual loves himself as his mother once loved him.

It is important to point out that the seductress in this fantasy is not the homosexual's real mother, nor is she an image of the actual mother; it is a character he has imagined, based on his real mother. It is an ambiguous, dominating *persona*, half-motherly, half-virile, that we psychoanalysts call "the phallic mother". The homosexual identifies (or identifies his partner) with this phallic representation of the seducing mother.

I would like to mention here another interesting theory of the genesis of homosexuality. It could be summarized in terms of a recommendation addressed to therapists: "In the presence of a homosexual patient, think of his brother. And if he doesn't have a real one, think of his *virtual* brother". I believe that siblings play a major role in the genesis of homosexuality: the love given to the partner replicates the passionate love the homosexual felt for a brother—or, I should say, a brother who once was hated. It may seem complicated, but in the background history of homosexuals I generally find that the following schema applies: first, feelings of hostility towards the brother-rival, then love for this same brother, then, finally, homosexual love. That is why I would say that male homosexuality has to do with the transformation of an erstwhile hatred for a brother into love for another man.

As to homosexual women, I would say there are two types. Those who assert their homosexuality very early on in life—from about age twelve—will never change and will never experience heterosexuality. Then there are those who begin by being hetero-sexual, then are lesbian for some time, before reverting to heterosexual relationships.

Women in the first group are masculine-looking, and have never had heterosexual intercourse; they have a deep disgust for anyone who has a penis. They loathe men, as they imagine them to be brutal, contemptuous, cowardly, and boastful. But it must be understood that their rejection of men-as-sexual-beings is not a rejection of masculinity as such. Quite the contrary; they idealize masculinity and want it for themselves. They experience themselves as refined masculine beings, perfect in all respects, stripped of all the defects that men have and by far superior to men in general.

The ideal being with whom they identify is in fact a hybrid character made up of a masculine part and a maternal part—a kind of strange masculinized mother, simultaneously powerful and protective.

These lesbian women seem to adjust their love life to suit an imaginary scene in which they play the part of the masculinized mother and have their partner play the complementary role of an innocent little doleful-eyed girl who has to be tenderly protected.

The other type of female homosexuality, quite different from the first, could be described as more feminine in nature. Such a woman has had heterosexual experiences, she is more often than not married, and may even have children, but she falls madly in love with another woman, strong and gentle at the same time—a woman who possesses both masculine attributes and maternal qualities. When the passion burns out, such women may well rediscover the pleasure of being in a heterosexual relationship.

To put it simply, we could say, therefore, that there are two types of homosexual women: in the one case, they identify with a man who is sexless and has maternal aspects; in the other, they identify with a little girl in need of protection.

In both cases, however, what strikes me as the crucial point in the homosexual link between two women is that it is built upon feelings of infinite tenderness, nostalgia, and mutual weakness. Two men come together around an erect penis; but two women love each other in order to taste, as Colette (1927) put it, "the bitter delight of feeling similar, insignificant and forgotten".

CHAPTER EIGHT

The presence of males in abortion discourse and practices[1]

Juan-Guillermo Figueroa-Perea

Introduction

The aim of this article is to propose certain reflections on the *different kinds of participation* that males have in the interruption of a pregnancy, both in the practice of abortion *per se* and in defining norms and criteria for it. The complexity of this issue stems, in the first place, from the fact that males play a *secondary role as subjects* that reproduce; for that reason, they are not informants sought out by several disciplines when attempting to reconstruct the population's reproductive experiences. Rather, identifying their characteristics and behaviours is useful mostly for determining the manner in which they influence women's reproduction and the economic stratification of the populations in which analyses are conducted.

To a certain extent, it is assumed that it is right to consider women as the persons most closely responsible for biological reproduction, while men are identified as actors in processes involving social reproduction. On the basis of these assumptions, information is produced to support strategies for social organization in the sphere of reproductive behaviours, and thus differential strategies are generated for dealing with men and women.

Taking into account that this is the reference used in most cases, one of the lines I would like to pursue in this article is to propose several hypotheses on the reasons why males are a secondary actor in models for interpreting reproduction and also to discuss how that produces conceptual lacunae, practical ambiguities, and confusion in the process of defining reproductive rights and responsibilities, despite the fact that, at the same time, males are identified as relevant actors for defining moral discourse intended to regulate the possibility of abortion. In other words, it is in the sphere of social reproduction where social norms are usually defined and where mechanisms are set up for monitoring and following them up, regardless of the fact that said norms have repercussions on biological reproduction.

Abortion in the context of socio-demographic research on fertility

In demographic research on reproduction, a number of components have been privileged as tools for interpreting the basic dynamic processes included in this discipline. Analyses are made, on the one hand, of fertility levels and, on the other, of the individual behaviours and contextual features that may account for the variations found among the offspring of different social groups.

One of the models most widely used to provide a breakdown of the components of fertility levels is the intermediate variable model (Davis & Blake, 1956). Within this model, characteristics are defined that have a bearing on exposure to the risk of having intercourse, the risk of subsequent conception, and finally on whether pregnancies reach term. In each of these three groups, a search has been made for variables that discriminate, more closely, between the differences in fertility levels; some of the relevant factors that have been defined are contraception, breastfeeding, abortion, and the duration of marriage (Potter, 1982).

Another procedure has been to analyse those variables as behaviours to be explained in and of themselves; along these lines, there are analytical studies on the determinants of contraception, breastfeeding, and abortion. Different analytical exercises have broken them down in terms of the individual characteristics of the person reproducing and those of her partner, while also taking into account the influences of family members or persons in other groups to which they belong, as well as the effects of other social actions, such as health programmes (Mundigo & Indriso, 1999).

However, when attempts are made to determine the role males have played in different models for demographic interpretation, one finds that, in most, the idea is still upheld that women are the ones who are reproducing, that males play a secondary role and that, therefore, they should be analysed as an influence on processes affecting women rather than as being jointly responsible for reproduction. Only recently have there been efforts to try to develop indicators on reproductive processes in which males participate in a relational way with women and, thus, are not only included as part of the independent or intermediate variables for fertility and its determinants, but also within the very object of study that one wishes to interpret (Greene & Biddlecom, 2000; Figueroa, 1998).

The secondary presence of males in the analysis of reproduction has had consequences in the form of oversimplifications that are generated when interpreting certain stages of reproduction, but also in the type of policies and programmes that are defined to try to regulate fertility through the development of a greater number of contraceptive methods for women (as an example of this), as well as the so-called "maternal–child health programmes", within which we usually find follow-up of pregnancy, delivery and the puerperium, the prevention of unwanted pregnancies, and the treatment of complications associated with abortion. Ironically, that validates the concept that males do not reproduce or rather, that their role and presence is marginal. Nevertheless, at the same time there is a perception of "little male involvement" and of a lack of equality in the type of responsibilities that are assumed in the sphere of reproduction. For that reason, some feminist researchers and activists have come to question the assumptions utilized to interpret and establish social norms for the components of reproduction.

One of the major issues questioned has to do with the type of authors that are identified in the establishment of norms. That is to say, if women have been the main protagonists of reproduction, both in terms of how different disciplines interpret their role and how they assign responsibilities in experiencing the effects of reproduction and in following-up its different stages, why, then, would it seem that social and institutional norms derive from male authorities, with androcentric elements, in which the way that the specific experiences of women are taken into account is not only far from obvious, but also tends to be contradictory?

It is paradoxical that the individuals who are establishing norms for the different stages involved in reproduction and are authorizing matters related to abortion, are social actors perceived to be removed from the reproductive process. On the other hand, they are individuals whose gender identity is constructed around the fact that they are to be encouraged to create norms for others and lead others, in many instances without getting involved themselves, without questioning themselves about these norms on an individual basis, without talking about themselves (Seidler, 1997) and, in particular, validating and reproducing differential behaviour codes for men and women (Hierro, 1990).

Due to the repercussion they have in reflections concerning abortion, it would be worthwhile to focus on instances of learning and reproducing distinct norms in the experience of sexuality, since, in the case of women, they are encouraged to experience sexual intercourse as a function of reproduction, and to strive towards satisfying the male partner. However, in the case of males, the kind of sexuality that is encouraged is competitive, violent, used as a resource for domination and subjugation, homophobic, and is accustomed to not being held accountable for either its effects or consequences, even though males are encouraged to boast about their sexual encounters (Hernández, 1995; Szasz, 1998).

Another important dimension of these underlying differential codes associated with reproduction has to do with the kinds of experiences individuals have in the realm of health and illness; since males are encouraged to seek out situations involving risks and are also "taught" to look down upon the care of their own body, they at times reach a point that has been classified as "suicidal negligence" (Bonino, 1989; De Keijzer, 1995). In the case of women, they are morally disempowered, because they are expected to devote their lives to others, taking care of others (including those who fail to take care of themselves) and only looking out for themselves "in the time left over" (Basaglia, 1984; Sayavedra & Flores, 1997). Due to these behaviour patterns which individuals are taught, the major causes of death among males are violent situations and those arising from drunkenness derived from their learned gender role. As for women, there are many instances in which they do not take proper care of themselves because they feel they do not have the right to do so or because they lack the time to do so. For them, many causes of death or morbidity are associated with their reproductive function, which is idealized by society.

Although the preceding description of men and women's sexual practices and health care appears to be too "clear cut", the situations mentioned above arise frequently; the number of men and women who die due to the causes referred to above is high enough to make those the most important causes of death. It is necessary to delve into the impact that these types of sexual experiences and others involving caring (or not caring) properly for oneself have as a moral referent and as a valuational assumption for constructing norms regarding certain reproductive events, such as abortion.

We should ask ourselves: what kind of norms can be constructed from a male perspective concerning a reproductive event when the members of our society have come to learn that males do not reproduce; when, in addition, males have learned not to be accountable for their sexual practices; when they have learned to abuse their own bodies and those of others instead of caring for them; when they have learned that taking care of one's body is a sign of weakness; when they have learned that motherhood would appear to be the obligatory fate of women, whereas fatherhood is a luxury for males; when it is often acknowledged that females' sexuality should be geared toward reproduction and, therefore, they should assume the consequences; when in many cases it is recognized that men are the only ones who can separate sexuality from reproduction, as opposed to women; and when, in the last analysis, many males are not used to negotiating sexist norms that lead to gender inequalities, especially when it would seem that the benefits of reproducing outweigh the disadvantages? This issue is even more complex because, from time immemorial, the presence of males as authority figures tends to be repeated and justified in social institutions and norms.

While the questions posed above are somewhat rigid, the idea is to show some of the contradictory and ambivalent situations that should be taken into account when attempting to achieve a comprehensive view of the presence of males in the sphere of reproduction and in norms regarding abortion. The intention is not to "satanize" males, but rather to gain insights into their presence on the basis of the reproductive, sexual, and gender experiences of those who are reproducing.

Sociopolitical aspects and the use of language regarding abortion

An example of the complex and ambivalent presence of males in reproductive processes can be found when researching the topic of abortion, since it is framed within a reflection on reproductive rights and, at the same time, as an object of moral, penal, and social sanctions. Studies conducted in Brazil show that men have a more liberal, permissive discourse when they speak about their own sexuality in contrast to women, in whose case the attitude towards talking about these matters appears to be more conservative and subject to possible sanctions. However, when discussing abortion, males are more conservative and take a position denying the possibility that abortion may be recognized as part of women's rights to self-determination in the sphere of reproduction. Women, on the other hand, claim abortion as a prerogative in their reproductive process, undoubtedly because they feel more involved in reproduction and more closely affected by it and the unwanted consequences of their sexuality (Leal & Fachel, 1995).

In a study on opinions and social representations concerning abortion and contraception among males in Havana, Cuba (García, n.d.), it was found that one of the components related to abortion and males is that abortion is an event that always refers to another person; in other words, something that is constructed from the discourse and perception of others since it is not expressed or felt as a personal experience of males.

This moral appraisal, which differs between men and women, is confirmed in Mexico, where the findings of Núñez and Palma (1991) indicated that adolescent males state that an abortion has occurred, more often than females, possibly because the males are sanctioned, morally and legally, to a lesser extent. In addition, there are cases of males who state they are unaware of the outcome of pregnancies in which they know they have been involved; evidently, they are used to not being held accountable for consequences of their sexual lives.

In a study done in Colombia it was found that women assume from the very start that men will not accept their decision to have an abortion, which explained, in many cases, why males are not aware that their regular partner has decided to have an abortion. In general, they describe their decision-making processes with occasional partners or persons with whom they have a relationship that is not accepted socially. This has led to a dual silence that takes the form of a highly-marked relational imbalance in which both actors (women and men) refuse to speak in the presence of their partner (Salcedo, 1999).

When discussing the role of men in the decision to have an abortion, Tolbert and Morris (1995) exemplify how the different models for gender relations can influence the range of decisions that are made about abortion: the greater the equality between men and women in the different spheres of social activity, the greater the transparency in negotiations between them concerning abortion; however, little research has been done in this regard.

Language, discourse, and gender norms

One of the aspects that has been successfully documented by linguistic research is that as human beings learn ways of naming and ordering reality, we learn and come to acknowledge as evident certain categories for assessing reality, establishing hierarchies, and taking a stand regarding this. The nuances we fail to name would appear to go unseen, the differences that do not become evident in discourse often are not obvious in one's vision of reality, and valuational classifications that are combined and confused with terms for identifying objects, persons, and situations in reality, are frequently introjected even before the individual develops a verbal or written language.

That leads to a cognitive process and the acquisition of resources for participating in that process are quite sexist in nature, given how pervasive these are in the organization of society. An example of this are the ways of referring to and defining males or the male population in contrast to women; in many instances, males are described in relation to themselves, while, in contrast, women are referred to by society in relation to men. Castro and Bronfman (1993) document sexist features of medical discourse when physicians and other medical personnel account for the physiological events experienced by men and women and the interplay of roles in medical encounters, depending on whether the actors are male or female. Thus, many authors have come to the conclusion that, rather than a differential process of naming things and reality according to an individual's biological sex, said process arises in the gender specialization models we are exposed to as human beings in terms of the genitals we were born with (Lagarde, 1994).

Different male and female authors have shown how such language learning experiences are associated with differential ways of assuming and assessing reality. Seidler (1989, 1997) identifies males as individuals used to naming reality, within a logic of assigning it terms in order to describe and classify it, but at the same time reluctant to name themselves, to speak about themselves; and yet they are most willing to develop discourses referring to others. Thus, moral reasoning processes tend to be more rigid among males, due to their criterion for reviewing the compliance of norms in more abstract or deontological terms (Lamas, 1993; Sánchez Vázquez, 1996), as the persons who define norms and, therefore, evaluate whether behaviour patterns conform to them or not, often disregarding individuals' contexts, nuances, and real conditions for putting a norm into practice but also for expressing their opposition to it when they disagree with it.

On the other hand, it is necessary to mention a book by Gilligan (1982) that is most significant in terms of ethics and morals viewed from a feminist perspective. Although this text has been challenged by some, it has also been reread and cited constantly, since it illustrates some of the aspects of the relationship between gender learning processes and the construction of moral reasoning (Madrid, 1993). Gilligan identifies variants in the way in which women construct moral arguments and refers to an ethic of care. The main point of discussion is the origin of differences between men and women regarding the way they sustain moral judgments. That is to say, is it in one's essence, in one's nature, or is it due to the above-mentioned learning process? Could it be possible that males are exposed to a learning process fostering personal neglect (De Keijzer, 1995) and geared to directing others and establishing norms for them (Seidler, 1997)?

What Gilligan documents is a valuational reference constructed, in women, more from a logic of care than from that of strict compliance with norms. This evidences certain similarities with teleological positions (Lamas, 1993; Sánchez Vázquez, 1996) in which contexts are important, since the motives for behaviours and the conditions under which such behaviours take place produce nuances in values and make them more flexible. This has significant consequences in topics such as abortion, experienced closely by women and at more of a distance by men, even though the latter are acknowledged as moral authorities when norms are established in this regard. Hence, the importance of delving more deeply into some of the elements of males' normative discourse.

Feminism has documented that gender relations make dialogue between men and women more difficult and complex because males tend to doubt the legitimacy of the language used by women and claim that it is emotional, while at the same time their own language is constructed on the basis of the notion of authority. In this context, reason becomes a sign of civilization; however, this sign is presented as the dominant masculinity identified with self-control and rational sex. Males often learn to express themselves and to use language as a means of defence against feelings and against contact, because both of these threaten the notion of masculinity.

The structure of emotional life, in relation to discourse, is conditioned by gender and, thus, language can be used to control and attenuate emotion, with the idea of not feeling and in order not to express oneself. In gender relations, many males find it hard to communicate through negotiation because, traditionally, their vision as a source of authority may come into play; on the other hand, this may mean that certain emotions and feelings are inaccessible for males, both in their learned ability to experience them and in the legitimized possibility of expressing them.

Seidler suggests the need to clarify contradictions among the language, experiences, discourse, and emotional lives of males; until now, these elements have not been sufficiently documented in social research.

Some reflections for a tentative conclusion

Despite the contradictions in norms and practices related to abortion, women have disregarded punitive legislation, social norms, and internal emotional pressures, and have decided to have an abortion as an extreme alternative in the face of an unwanted pregnancy. They have thus assumed more active attitudes and have taken actions involving resistance to social norms, discourses, and practices and abortion has become a transgressive phenomenon in which we have yet to properly document males' experiences.

An important component in this analytical inquiry consists of redefining research objectives and questions on the basis of the particular concept we have of reproduction and what the presence of males in the reproductive process means. The first option involves considering reproduction as something that is germane to women. In other words, it is part of the dynamic processes that are their business, their responsibility, processes that they experience physiologically and that, moreover, they may suffer the consequences of that experience under risk conditions. This leads to identifying males as secondary actors who may collaborate actively and positively, or rather, hinder and obstruct processes experienced by women. A second line of interpretation is related to considering males as actors in reproduction, as subjects who are reproducing through the links they establish with their body and with other bodies, not only in heterosexual encounters but with persons of their own sex.

The second analytical line of interpretation seems more consistent to me, and within that line of interpretation I propose that studies be conducted on how males in different social contexts relate to their own bodies and also to the bodies of their partners (female or male), since numerous research efforts have documented the lack of care that many males evidence for those bodies. This undoubtedly has a bearing on the exercise of their reproductive rights and on those of women.

I ask myself—along with the feminists—what would those norms be like if men were the ones who got pregnant. Rather than seeing this as an idle, useless hypothetical situation, it is in fact a criticism of the lack of sensitivity in norms with regard to women's experiences. Besides, I am sure that if males experienced the problems that women do, the norms would surely be drastically different.

Note

1. Summarized version of a paper presented at the Sixth National Meeting on Demographic Research in Mexico, Mexico City, August, 2000. This chapter was originally published as part of an article published in the journal *Papeles de Poblacion*, No 25, July–September 2000.

CHAPTER NINE

The sexed body and the real— its meaning in transsexualism

Leticia Glocer Fiorini & Águeda Giménez de Vainer

Introduction

I n psychoanalysis, theoretical notions concerning the body are particularly relevant and remain a subject of debate. There are many planes involved in the concept of body. On the one hand, there are the meanings assigned to the body in clinical practice: the body of hysteria and of psychosomatic illness, the body of the actual nucleus of the neuroses, the body of transsexualism, all present specific problems. On the other hand, there are the meanings attached and attributed to the body by the cultural discourse of each historical moment.

All subjects construct a specific relationship with their body on the basis of meanings given by the parents' discourses and desires, which intersect with a body that has drives. The relation between the anatomic body, the erogenous body, and the meanings constructed by individuals, structures a complex field that brings together many variables, none of which should be ignored.

The sexed body raises some of the most relevant questions in psychoanalysis. How is the sexed body constituted? How does it influence the processes of subjectivation? Is the sexed body a factor that puts order into an itinerary and sets a limit to processes related to access to the difference between the sexes? Or is it an envelope-support that can be modified to the point of the possibility of radically changing sex or sexed identity?

In this sense, transsexualism presents the question of the sexed body as a major problem. It also brings up broader problems: the role of the real body in sexuation and, in essence, challenges us to work on the delimitations of this concept.

One of the great questions that transsexualism raises is whether sexual identity can be changed by adjusting the anatomic sex to fit an identity conviction by means of surgery. Can transsexuals tread this path and adapt, without major conflicts, to a previously fantasied identity? Can a man become a woman, in the manner of Virginia Woolf's Orlando? Can these physical transformations refer to changes in sexuality, and on the itineraries of desire? In this sense, the subject of the body overflows the frame of transsexualism, but is also a particularly appropriate angle from which to approach this problem.

Transsexuals have the absolute conviction of belonging to the gender opposite to the one assigned to him or her at birth. It is a far more radical rejection than simply assuming some stereotyped sexual roles. There is a feeling of incongruence between the biological sex and the assigned gender, although they have neither anatomical nor hormonal anomalies; they are neither hermaphrodites nor pseudo-hermaphrodites.

There are different theories on transsexualism regarding their nosological situation: disturbance of gender identity, structural psychosis, a paranoid delusion localized in the sexual identity.

Stoller (1968) borrows the concept of sex–gender dissociation that was previously developed in the field of anthropology. He gives the notion of core gender identity the position of a major and basic determinant. The transsexual suffers a gender pathology the resolution of which could be to adapt his biological sex to his conviction of being a woman.

Laplanche (1980) argues against this conceptualization, asking why one of the terms in the sex–gender system is placed on the side of anatomy and the other on the side of psychology. He proposes that "sex should be defined as the set of physical or psychic determinations, behaviour, fantasms, directly linked to sexual function and pleasure; gender is the set of physical or psychic determinations, behaviour, fantasms, linked to the distinction between male and female."

Faure-Oppenheimer (1980) considers that "choice of sex" is not independent of physical determinations.

This debate includes a basic discussion referring to: first, whether gender identity is a major determinant in the processes of subjectivation and sexuation; second, the place of sexuality in the frame of the sex–gender system.

We recall that Freud (1920a) postulated a series of factors that work together in multiple permutations: anatomic traits, male or female psychic characters, and object choice. He points out that not all of these coincide concordantly in the same individual. This refers to the formation of complex structures, as Morin (1990) suggests in his discussion of complex thought.

Clinical reference: a male transsexual

We discuss part of a clinical vignette already published (Giménez de Vainer & Glocer Fiorini, 1995) as a basis for reflection on the place of the real body in the processes of subjectivation and sexuation.

A subject consults as a transsexual who had surgery seventeen years previously. His appearance and physical attitudes are those of a woman, though the tone of voice and muscle development seem discordant. His objective is for the psychoanalyst to recognize his new sexual identity for legal reasons. He had undergone multiple operations, which consisted not only in the genital transformation but also surgeries of the nose, ankles, chin, and compulsive depilation of the whole body. He says, "I know I'm a man genetically and I have a man's strength ... And I can use it if necessary ..." His "knowledge" does not coincide with his absolute conviction of being a woman.

In the interviews, there is an anxious tone that he attributes to lack of social recognition of his present identity, sustained by his firm conviction of "being" a woman. This generated contained aggressiveness on the verge of exploding, linked to a fracture of his narcissistic unity—his real body and his sexual identity in a conflict-ridden struggle.

A point of special interest was that, although he introduced himself as a woman, he feared being found out through blood tests, such as those required for job interviews, or because his muscles were better developed than is usual in women. His daily life was perturbed by persecutory episodes in relation to the fear that his "other identity" might be discovered. In one of these episodes, he had been bitten by a dog, and this unleashed an uncontainable state of automatic anxiety, when he assumed that he should go to an emergency room and that his former identity would be discovered. The anxiety generated takes the forms of castration anxiety, but is an automatic anxiety beyond the frame of neurotic anxiety.

The meaning of the act

We would like to highlight two aspects in relation to sex change in the transsexual, in the first place, to try to determine how the subject reaches the act of transformation. This act involves the search for a sanction of the new identity that affects a key point: sexual identity. There is an ideal, embodied in the feminine; there is a search for an "aesthetic" ideal and, in this sense, female forms have a fundamental role.

Therefore, this act of transformation is double faced: on one side, the wish for a form—aesthetics heavy with meaning that the subject has localized in his body; on the other side, the mutilation and neo-construction of another sexed body, an act that masks and tries to organize primary anxieties and death anxieties connected with being.

A female body is constructed in an attempt to adapt it to the absolute and un-modifiable conviction of being a woman. In this sense, the body is interpreted as a de-erogenized envelope, simply an article of clothing that could be changed without major consequences. The limits between the real body and the clothing fade (Kaplan, 1991). The subject seeks other wrappings, another ego; it is a neo-constructed body. Of course, genetic sex cannot be changed; a disavowed mark remains in the subject that is part of a process of farther-reaching splittings. This disavowal is supported precisely by the enthronement of the body envelope as a point of inflection for the sex change. This also suggests the relations between the body as envelope, as apparel and as disguise. The disguise is an acquisition whose symbolic value is to permit, on certain regulated occasions, the acquisition of "another Ego", even another sexual identity. In the case of the transsexual who has had surgery, the disguise loses its playful character and is frozen into a sometimes caricaturesque mould.

We recall that for Freud (1923b) the ego is primarily a body ego. This implies considering the real body and the meanings attached to it in the form of imaginary identifications that constitute an ego. We include Castoriadis-Aulagnier's concept (1975) of the mother as spokeswoman for social discourse and basically, for an identificatory project that interacts with the drive body.

In the second place, the act of transformation involves a mutilation with the participation of a third party who sanctions the operation. This participation by a third party does not mean that it is not a self-mutilation. However, it is important to point out that in the unfolding of this act, the transsexual is not a subject, but rather the object of an Other's scene.

The creation of a scene that takes shape is needed to sanction a new identity. However, it is not a hysteric scene, with symbolic and metaphoric value. On the contrary, it is an attempt to solve gender and sexual dilemmas that can ultimately end in mutilation, real castration, and death. In the case mentioned, in the patient's words, after the operation, the surgeon masturbates him by rubbing the neo-formed "clitoris". The patient has an orgasm and the physician says, "Now you're a woman."

This poses a major problem: how to cathect a neo-body that has not been marked by a libidinal history of erogenization? We know, that for all subjects, the body is evidence of a libidinal genealogy, with meanings that date back to initial maternal care and are re-signified by the oedipal process.

It is worthwhile to question whether the construction of a receptive space, in the manner of a cul de sac, is equivalent to the meanings ascribed to the vagina in the girl's theory of the cloaca? Or whether the reduction of the size of the penis is equivalent to the libidinal marks of the clitoris, in its genealogy as an erogenous zone? Considering these dilemmas, we think that in the process of transformation, this neo-constructed body must become a fetish, supported by a structural disavowal. In the case mentioned, this develops in the frame of the rite of initiation whose scene is created by the physician.

In the case of the transsexual who has had surgery, part of the body is mutilated in search of an ideal construction or a neo-construction that is part of the fantasy of constructing another subject, another sex. He imagines a new starting point, based on a process of eternalization. Pallingenesis, which refers to eternal rebirth from the subject's own ashes, is an atemporal fantasy of eternity (Assoun, 1989). This fantasy is supported by exacerbated and omnipotent narcissism. The transsexual's act of transformation embodies a massive identification with the Mother: she is, imaginarily, a phallic, all powerful mother; therefore, the transsexual's transformation involves an exacerbation of phallicism. In this sense, the sex change operation, and consequent anatomical feminization, mask and also reveal phallicism incarnated in the body.

We may also wonder whether there might be a subjacent fantasy of procreation. Just as God created Eve from Adam's rib, the transsexual tries to create (to pro-create) a woman out of a man whose conviction is that he is a woman. In trying to access what no man could do, he takes the myth to its ultimate consequences. This appears in a social context where biotechnology produces unimagined achievements in the field of assisted fertilization and cloning. The possibility of creating life outside the sexual union of the couple (virgin pregnancies, children without the mother's respective pregnancy) are part of the context in which these transformations take place, since it provides them with an imaginary substrate. In this frame, the infantile sexual theories contribute their own themes.

Interaction is established between the ideal female body that is wished for and the mutilated body, the body of horror, that provokes death anxieties. Thus, the search for a female identity is supported by masochistic jouissance, by something "beyond the pleasure principle" (Freud, 1920b).

We can interpret that a script takes shape and that, instead of being narrated in the neurotic style, it becomes present in an act. There is a strategy with the participation of physician and patient, whose core is disavowal and rejection of the symbolic difference. In the case of the transsexual, the script is written by an Other; who perhaps embodies trans-generational mandates to which the subject has no symbolic access.

In this interaction, the creation of a new body, in an attempt to adapt it radically to a previously assumed and fantasied sexual identity, tends to calm and organize, in different degrees, a psyche overflowing with anxiety. For Millot (1983), the sex change operation has a replacement effect that can avoid psychotic crisis.

We will now return to the initial question: "is the real body a contingent element that could be modified in order to stabilize a structure?" Faure-Oppenheimer (1980) emphasizes that the reality of the sexed body forms a limit, that it constitutes borders and indicates the limits of the processes of construction of a sexual identity.

Comments

Diverse planes come together and lead to the postulation that there is no pure anatomic body; the sexed body of the newborn is cathected and signified on the basis of parental desires and discourses, mainly the mother's and then the father's. The drive body cathects prioritized erogenous zones, it becomes an imaginary, fantasmatic body, an object of desire, cathected and signified by the field of an Other.

In this context, the real body forms a limit that signals a specificity. There is no absolute contingency, there are no arbitrary meanings, the processes of subjectivization do not go down an open or infinite path. There is no arbitrariness in this transit; the materialness of the sexed body with its meanings is a definite limit and is *one* of the factors that outlines the itineraries in sexuation. *There is no "free" sex choice, even though sexuality can be exercised freely.* The body is not a simple prop that can be changed without consequences, although in certain cases, as we said, this operatory may attenuate unbearable anxiety. It is an extremely problematic act from the psychoanalytic perspective, even though it may provide a relief and a means to reach some kind of temporary psychic organization.

Gender identity must also be differentiated from sexuality. *Gender identity is not a major determinant, but rather one element in a complexity.* It is based on gender identifications, ideals, to be constructed from birth on the basis of an identificatory project that is later symbolized in the oedipal process. But we must point out that in the sex–gender pair, the field of the drive and of sexuality are not clearly included. *Also, we must not forget that each subject is inhabited by masculine and feminine phantasms, independent of his or her anatomy and sexual identity.*

The theoretical problems and challenges posed by transsexualism are not foreign to the frame of sexual indifferentiation, androgyny and bisexuality that are pertinent to today's socio-cultural contexts. These contexts can induce adjustments of the theory to new biotechnological offerings and new demands.

The discussion that we have developed inevitably leads to the question: what is a woman? What are the specificities differentiating a woman born as such who symbolically takes a feminine position in her singularity (beyond gender stereotypes), a transsexual who must transform his body in order to adapt it to his firm conviction of being a woman, and a transvestite who dresses up as a woman, but would never accept a mutilation of his penis?

Laplanche (1980) distinguished the logic of gender diversity from the logic of sexual differentiation. We postulate that *many of the problems connected with transsexualism are played out within the logic of diversity, beyond the strict binarities, while the plane of the symbolic difference between the sexes is excluded.*

In view of these challenges, one of us (Glocer Fiorini, 1998, 2001) proposed

> the need to consider the relations between the three registers ultimately heterogeneous but coextant: 1) anatomic heterogeneity and its meanings in the male–female pair; 2) gender diversity in the processes of imaginary identification relevant to masculinity and femininity, leading to sexual identity and 3) the symbolic difference between the sexes in the broader development of the field of desire. Between these three registers, their conjunctions and disjunctions, there are zones of intersection. In these zones other laws and other phenomena are generated that differ from those corresponding to the original categories.

This means using the contributions of complex thought, beyond the false options or limitations of monocausal thought. The way these registers operate together depends on the kind of defences functioning. From repression to disavowal, different variations of subjectivation are generated, and these are more or less problematic and conflictive for each subject.

CHAPTER TEN

Masculinity revisited: a self-deconstruction[1]

John Munder Ross

I t is now about ten years since I last wrote about men and collected my contributions on the subject in a book distilling two decades of work on it—*What Men Want* (Ross, 1994). Instead of generalizations about themes such as fatherhood and masculinity, I have since turned my attention more to form than to content in psychic life. That is, to the nature of therapeutic action at critical and mutative moments in the analytic process and to our history and the influence of subjective and extrinsic factors on our theorizing and subsequent technique.

It is in the spirit of the latter, of understanding why we choose to believe what we do at any given time, that I will now revisit and deconstruct my earlier research and conceptual reflections on male development. A retrospective of this sort, acknowledging the biases in one's own work, may be painful at times. However, examinations of our psychoanalytic past, and consequent epistemology, are essential to the viability of our field's future.

* * *

At the end of the twenty years in question, from roughly 1970 until 1990, I came to stress what I believed to be two polar forces in the psychology of men. I emphasized their bedrock femininity on the one hand, and, on the other, their equally innate and unfolding aggressivity. In conflict with each other, both sets of imperatives are, I further concluded, subject to all sorts of societally driven constraints, intrapsychic anxieties and consequent tensions and inhibitions. I wrote (1994, pp. 12–13):

> The tensions men experience—which derive from their basic instinctual drives, their sexuality and aggression, and from their relations with others—constantly impinge in paradoxical ways on men's sense of masculinity. As much as men *will* be men, as ingrained as their male destiny is, they must constantly contend with contradictory forces within themselves.
>
> First of all, men also wish to be like women sometimes, or rather the way they see women. Unconsciously at least, they long to have and to be charmed by children, to be passive, sexy, sensuous, feminine. Most men have been brought up by their mothers so that the first significant others in their lives, their models for being a person, were female. Their mothers' female aura, to borrow from Robert Stoller (1975), has left a deep imprint on their son's psyches. So, later on in life, women's womanliness tends to seem both awesome and catching. Be with women, men fear, or do what they do, and they risk becoming female.
>
> Men's psychological masculinization is analogous to the fetal androgynization that takes place in the womb. They begin their emotional lives in the orbit of women, whom they are like in many respects. Like hormones, psychological male principles have to be introduced into their experience and their psyches if they are to feel like men one day. In the case of the mind, it is largely the father who is the agent of a boy's masculine development. A consideration of fathers, like mothers before them, is essential to an understanding of the psychology of men. And one of the major characteristics associated with fathers, as with all adult males, is their propensity to display aggression and invite identifications in kind with their ability to do harm.
>
> Thus, on the other side of the coin, men feel terrified of the haunting potential for violence that seems to go with being male. They recoil from the physical destructiveness they sense in themselves and other men. Aggression in men figures as a survival mechanism serving the community. Impelled by their testosterone, males were

made to fight, and they are taught to do so by other men, notably their fathers. More than this, being aggressive for most men means being male, and they can exploit their hostility to reassure themselves that they are. The trouble is, their violence can also get out of hand.

Baffled by his female patients and colleagues, Freud is said to have once asked his disciple and benefactor, Princess Marie Bonaparte, "My God, what does woman want?" Men, we now know, are no less mysterious.

Even today in a changed psychoanalytic universe, in which we tend to discard factitious norms and therefore the developmental lines that presumably coalesce to actualize them, these generalizations ring true—at least to me. The trouble is, that looking back, I can clearly see the personal and political motives that impelled my research along these lines. As much as any of the empirical evidence I found, these considerations and constraints further moved me to make the conclusions about this work that I did.

Decorum constrains me from getting too personal when it comes to my individual history and inner life, except to say that we psychoanalysts often write about our core conflicts in attempts to master and normalize them, though few of us tend to acknowledge this (Erik Erikson and Allen Wheelis are exceptions). However, the socio-cultural trends and situational demands that bear on our ideas require explication if our discipline is to do its job responsibly and continue to grow realistically, rather than wishfully. Once again, I will try to apply some notions about the "politics of theory" to my own history.

Eternal feminine

It was 1971 when I began my research on male development. A graduate student at what was then the country's premier clinical psychology programme at New York University—one which was heavily influenced by psychoanalytic notions and which, alas, is now defunct—I was casting about for a dissertation topic. Besides the inevitable unconscious motives that came to bear on my choice of topic, other conflicting forces came into play.

For one thing, there was my particular psychoanalytic heritage, alive and well at N.Y.U.'s Research Center For Mental Health under the aegises of George Klein, Merton Gill, and Robert Holt. I would work with all of them as I had with Erik Erikson as my tutor at Harvard College. Committed to investigating *empirically* Freud's and later psychoanalytic basic hypotheses, nonetheless all were, in their various ways, mavericks when it came to toeing its party line. They had paid the price for their heresies to one degree or another, finding themselves marginalized from the mainstream and the metapsychology that had been the staple of their apprenticeships. With their commitments to understanding the influence of historical, social, and cognitive actuality on psychic reality, like my psychoanalyst father before them, these iconoclasts served as my role models.

More generally, the women's movement, while not yet thoroughly ensconced in academia as it is today, was very much in the air. Its voice provided a clarion challenge to the authority of the gender stereotypes set forth by the psychoanalytic establishment. Indeed, the debacle of Vietnam, with which my whole generation had to contend, had called into question authority of any kind.

At the same time, I was planning to become a psychoanalyst. This meant that soon enough I would be entering the culturally and socially impregnable fortress of one or another of its institutes—a world apart. If I wanted to get in and get through—and this I did not quite tell myself—I would have to compromise.

And compromise I did. Rather than take on the Freudian canon and dispute, for example, the time-honoured notion of the primacy of penis envy in the development of femininity, I decided instead to search out its counterpart: "womb" or "baby envy" in boys and men. It seemed like such a new and challenging idea at the time, though I would soon learn it had been repeatedly asserted and forgotten. Indeed, questioning my ability to get results from conflict-laden boys, several potential sponsors turned me down. In the end, the independent minded Robert Holt, having dreamt of laying an egg after my presentation to him, took me on.

I have described elsewhere the large scale empirical project (n of 65) I devised to study the unfolding of childbearing and childrearing theories, fantasies, and wishes in boys from three- to ten-years-old and the unexpectedly significant results my statistical tests garnered. It seemed that most of the little boys I tested were far less fearful for their masculinity than the professional adult males whom I had consulted. Only over time would these children come to identify with their *fathers* as procreators and parents, paternal ambitions coming to replace increasingly fraught, and so less conscious, maternal ones.

Having broken this new ground, I would thereafter begin studies of a topic much neglected by the matrifocal theory then in its ascendancy (of Mahler, Bowlby, and Winnicott) and the research, often spearheaded by women, on children's pre-oedipal development. I would look at fathers, how they interact with sons and daughters in seemingly gender-specific ways throughout childhood, what they do for their children that is unique to their sex and how they as (mostly) young men conceptualize the role of the male parent.

In the meantime my findings and my conclusions about these observations, while seemingly radical, were still safe enough. Soft men, the "New Man", pleased the feminists who were more and more shaping a discipline that is now largely feminized. Nor was the challenge to the Freudian canon direct enough to raise too many eyebrows. Besides, the work still cleaved to the spirit of the developmental lines set forth by Anna Freud (1965).

Finally, it fell back on theoretical constructs, Weberian "ideal types", as if they were actual norms—a conceit all too characteristic of psychoanalysis up to that point in its history. With my burgeoning involvement in the fatherhood research that was the order of the day, I met the criteria for analytic training as a CORST candidate. I was on my way to a career as a researcher/teacher/ practitioner. All the while I told myself that I was merely seeking the truth.

Fatherhood and psychoanalytic training: struggles and lost opportunities

My observational research on what was then called "fathering" took place while I was doing my psychoanalytic training as the first psychologist matriculated at one of the American Psychoanalytic Association's most conservative institutes: Downstate, which moved to N.Y.U. Medical Center. I was also teaching clinical psychology at Ferkauf Graduate School, where I found students eager to participate with me in Judith Kestenberg's Child Development Research project. Kestenberg had found my initial work on men's core femininity congenial, having articulated her own views on what she called the "inner genital phase" in a boy's development. It was at Ferkauf that I also met Robert Stolorow, with whom I taught and with whom I wrote what appears to have been the first paper on intersubjectivity in clinical analysis (Stolorow *et al.*, 1978). The contrasts among the three settings, the "disconnects" to which they gave rise, and the roles they demanded of me were reflected in the work itself.

Like others in the fatherhood *movement* (which it nearly was), my own efforts were guided by an implicit sense of mission. The role of men in their children's lives had been ignored in developmental theorizing as it had been in the workplace. For example, psychoanalytic institutes, where young fathers were already removed from the home for so many hours of precious childrearing time, further tended to strip their mostly male candidates of their adult status and authority. And so, along with Lamb, Brazelton, and Yogman, and psychoanalysts Abelin and Herzog, I, too, stressed the critical importance of the "good enough" father in: (1) organizing his toddler's burgeoning sexual identity; (2) stimulating and then modulating the child's aggression; (3) serving as counterpoint to a potentially infantilizing mother; and, withal, completing the family picture.

Unlike more academic endeavours—my doctoral project, for example—the psychoanalytic observational research, of this era, was not particularly constrained in these days by methodologic checks and balances. (Mahler called the computer the "international b.m." machine. She relied instead on observer consensus as an informal version of inter-rater reliability.) These investigations tended to be anecdotal, selective and inevitably subjective in their culling and processing of evidence from which rather high order inferences were drawn. And thus it was easy enough to demonstrate, if not truly prove, the hypotheses that I had set forth and to fulfil less "scientific agenda".

How, then, to distinguish my work from that of non-analytic observers such as Yogman, Brazelton, and Lamb? It was here that I brought my new-found and evermore *clinical* identity to bear on my scrutiny of the behaviour of a father, anchoring his developmental role in *his* felt identity as a father. To observation I added the methodology of the in-depth interview (in the Vaillant and Coles tradition), drawing out of the men whom I and my assistants observed some of the same conflictual themes that I had discovered in my patients and indeed in myself as a new father (my son was born just as I began my training, teaching, and research). Struggles with infantile and maternal longings and the threat these posed to a man's somewhat tenuous maleness, guilt over oedipal triumph, the loss of one's own father, as what Peter Blos called protector and rescuer—all appeared to motivate what seemed to be typical interactions of fathers with their sons and daughters. Candidacy had steeped me in the unconscious, and now I saw it everywhere in daily life.

However, its peculiarities also confronted me with more troubling insights. As I began to present and publish in a multiciplicity of settings, realizing my need for recognition as an authority and thus as a mature man, I found myself increasingly dismayed by the authoritarianism to which I and my classmates were subjected by our self-appointed mentors—teachers, supervisors and, indeed, our assigned and reporting training analysts. It would be some time, indeed only when I had myself become a training analyst and a full professor, before I had the temerity to write directly about autocracy and sadomasochism in psychoanalytic organizations (Ross, 1999).

In the meantime, fortified by my colleague and sometime collaborator Jim Herzog's stress on men's aggressivity, I (re)discovered the so-called "Laius complex". "Oedipus Revisited" (first published in 1982 in *The Psychoanalytic Study of the Child*) was an oblique challenge to the status quo, political as well as theoretical, in psychoanalysis. In fact, as with men's feminine underbellies, analytic authors before me had written about the darker side of fatherhood, only to have their assertions repeatedly forgotten because of the resistances they aroused (Devereux; Kanzer; the Racovskys; Freud himself). They, too, had stressed the fact that King Laius, paradigmatic father of the Oedipus myth and complex, had been both a pederast and a would be filicide.

As much as they cherished children serving as the conduits of their "immortal germplasm", as Freud (1920b) had put it, none-theless, like Oedipus' doomed progenitor, all fathers seek to stave off death by wanting to rape, invade, and murder their offspring. Thus, all fathers—and all father *figures* in hierarchical organiza-tions—had to contend with unconscious sadomasochistic and murderous impulses toward their sons. In their crude form, these were certainly not "in the best interests of the child". However, reworked and modulated, like the Oedipus complex, the "Laius complex" might serve a child's development by moving fathers to stimulate and inevitably discipline and constrain their sons—and their daughters—in the service of socialization. Indeed, predictable sets of behaviour, expressing compromise formations in this vein, could be seen as the "releasors", in ethological terms, of the son's or daughter's oedipal phase.

In a literal sense, these views represented a revival, at a fraught time in psychoanalytic history, of Freud's "seduction hypothesis" and his traumatogenic theory of neurosis. Jeffrey Masson had just then "betrayed" Kurt Eissler and Anna Freud and had fallen from grace. More subtly, they suggested a complex and largely unconscious intersubjective dialogue between fathers and their children. This was at odds with both psychoanalysis' develop-mental overview and its theory of clinical technique. Remember, this was a time when adult development was discounted and when counter-transference was still felt to be a source merely of trouble rather than of information. Heralded as an innovative contribution by many psychoanalysts elsewhere, who had no self-interested stake in my submission within *their* dominance hierarchies, I found myself a "prophet without honour" in my own home. The more I wrote, the more marginalized I felt myself to be at my own institute, where, in contrast to the one then in power, virtually no one else of my generation—its capable candidates and recent graduates—dared to write papers of any sort much less challenge the theoretical status quo.

"Publish and perish", seemed the mantra of the junior analyst in the eras of my analytic training and of others before me. At best we might offer mere footnotes to Freud—Freud, as he was then taught. Freud as catechism. And so I was told by the old guard, quite literally, "Psychoanalysis has one complex. It doesn't need any more." Evidently, my efforts to understand and define masculinity in more intersubjective terms were bound up with those to maintain it in the face of psychoanalytic training.

*　　*　　*

"Freedom!" Jacob Arlow declared, "Freedom!" He, Herb Schlessinger, Arnold Cooper, and I were teaching a freewheeling elective at Columbia on "everything you wanted to know about psycho-analysis but were afraid to ask." On this particular morning, the candidates had asked us how we had experienced our graduations from the institutes where we had trained at our different points in generational time.

"I could think my own thoughts at last," Arlow continued, referring back to his emancipation from The New York Psycho-analytic in the 1940s and the id psychology of the refugee analysts ensconced in its seats of powers. Despite a forty-year span between them, our training experiences had not been dissimilar.

"Today you are a man," a classmate of mine declared at my private graduation party in 1984—the institute provided no such celebration and "infantile" gratification. He handed me a can of compressed tennis balls. "Here, you can have your balls back. I'm so envious!"

Romantic love and a breath of fresh air

Freed from the protracted apprenticeship and revived adolescence of candidacy, I did indeed feel somehow complete. With this, I would return from my expeditions into the grim violence of men's inter-generational struggles. Return, that is, to pleasure, to love, and to women.

Sudhir Kakar, the great psychoanalytic scholar of Hindu experience, also happened to be my oldest and closest, if geographically incorrect, friend. For two decades, he had, in writing and conversation, been introducing me to cross-cultural variations in the interplay between the sexes and to more explicit vagaries in his particular culture's definitions of gender. In India, bisexuality or, better, *ambi*sexuality (as Ferenczi dubbed it) was taken for granted—a given, built into the core of the mythology and extolled in the Sanskrit epics and ragas. He and I had also long shared the notion that the psychoanalysis we loved was nonetheless societally and historically bound and therefore constricting. Indeed, we had always felt that its world view and consequent developmental norms were very much those of the pre-war middle class Vienna imported into the American institutes it came to inhabit. What's more, now middle aged, we had once been young men together, had seen each other fall in and out of love and, back then, had talked into many a night about the self-revelations that came in the wake of youthful romance. Our discipline, we felt, had little to say about the sea change brought on by a man's first love.

Thus moved, Sudhir and I set about to explicate the paradigmatic love stories of our two literatures, adding to the mix those of the Perso–Islamic tradition. We did so primarily because of Nizami's sublime tale of "Layla and Majnun" (the madman), penned just at the time the troubadours of France first sang of Tristan and Isolde's tragic plight and of the prototypic western lover's more frank defiance of generational dominance and inner duty. Presaging Shakespeare's *Romeo and Juliet*, these twelfth-century love stories ended in the love death or "Liebestod" that Denis de Rougement had found at the mysterious core of an otherwise more secular and boundaried Western World. Through love, the wisdom of the East found its way into the European and Middle Eastern imaginations.

Seen in a psychoanalytic light, these *Tales of Love, Sex and Danger* (we published the book by this name in 1987) reflected back truths about the psychological nature and value of romantic, erotic love and its form of *unio mystica*—phenomena hitherto ignored because of the field's propensity to commit reductive genetic fallacies. Rooted in fraught pre-oedipal longings for symbiotic merger and for the feminine in both the other and the self, and made bittersweet because of the resonance with oedipal transgression and guilt, "genital" love (as it was then called) was also a developmental experience unto itself. Both finding himself in the arms of his woman and, in the process, failing to go about his "father's business" for a while, a young man might break free from his past in ways that the boy, whom he had been, could not.

First of all, equipped now with genital capacity (or "primacy" as it was called back then) and formal operational thought, he had the wherewithal both to experience sensual ecstasy and, decentring, to contemplate its illusory quality. Pre-adolescent boys, much less pre-oedipal or oedipal ones, were not mature enough for the madness of "first love". This was the "real thing", the "thing itself" in contrast to pregenital rehearsals for true love from bygone eras. Erotic and romantic love required the biological and cognitive maturation of adolescence. Down and dirty, expressed in the expression of bodily fluids, it was also spiritually transcendent.

Secondly, having united with a woman as a new and unique individual, the young lover identified with her person and perhaps with what Carol Gilligan called her sex's contextual ethic of care. Drinking her in, he also incorporated aspects of her value system. Her female "superego" (if you will) gentled the moral absolutes and categorical imperatives of his Freudian male conscience derived as this was from the paternal castration threat and thus suffused with the aggression of the Oedipus complex.

And so, first love helped boys become men, their own men. As he individuated from his father, the late adolescent lover might forge an "ego ideal" that was very much his own. It propelled young men toward an inner separation from their parents at the same as it completed them as whole people, indeed future fathers, in their own right.

Peter Blos saw this process of relinquishing what he called the "negative complex" as the final stumbling block en route to the internalized ego ideal, ontological solitude, and agency of an adult. To the mix we added the high frivolity of youthful ardour as the crucible for such a metamorphosis. When love was lacking in a man's life, something was missing in him. Every good clinician seemed to know this, searching for "the capacity to fall in love" in most consultations, but no one had quite articulated the developmental reverberations of its presence or absence (Person, Kernberg, and Bergman were exceptions).

Toward postmodernism

Radically challenging the then prevailing *emotional* conservatism of psychoanalysis, even these views of ours about men in love betrayed the field's, specifically ego psychology's, ever-present judgementalism and parochialism. To be sure, we had told ourselves, we were men, heterosexual men to boot, and could only speak honestly from our own subjective vantage and so not from a female or gay point of view.

Nonetheless, some disconcerting facts betrayed an unwanted chauvinism and heterosexism in our approach. For one thing, young women seemed to undergo much the same transformation in passion's wake and, when this failed to occur, a not dissimilar arrest in their individuation from their mothers. For another, feminists had increasingly challenged Gilligan's (then) dichotomization of "gendered" moral styles, seeing in her notions about ethical divergences not so much sex differences as individual ones. Finally, and perhaps most disconcerting, not a few of the poets and philosophers whom we had cited at length (notably, Auden and Barthes) were gay. Evidently, they had not needed encounters with women either to teach them about love or to grow up.

Realizations such as these moved me to reconsider the narrow-mindedness of my purview when I came to editing and concluding my final book on men in 1993. No doubt I was further affected by doing so in the community of international scholars and avant-garde artists collected at the Rockefeller Foundation's Villa Serbeloni in Bellagio. Reviving the pre-analytic flexibility of my interdisciplinary youth, I wrote (1994, pp. 205–206):

> ... I have found myself becoming more of a historical, cultural, and developmental relativist than I would have thought possible a generation ago. These days, particular variants interest me as much as universals or ideals.
>
> Femininity and masculinity are dynamic constructs, in other words, not simply biological givens. They are defined in terms of what they mean consciously and unconsciously to the individual. And, like any dimension of one's identity, male and female definitions of oneself represent syntheses, as Erikson himself might have noted, of biological disposition and endowment; the identifications and compromises that come with growing up in one particular family environment; and the roles and ideals that are afforded and valued by the surrounding society at any given point in its history. Though there are universal fantasies and wishes in the unconscious, so that a figure such as Oedipus seizes our imagination as he did in Sophocles' day, the meaning of being a woman or a man is complex, contextual, and variable. Being a man now, in 1994, is thus different from what it was for our fathers.

Moreover, a conventionality seemed to be built into the very notion of adult *development*, which in the 1980s had seemed so radical and liberating to psychoanalysts. In the absence of clearly defined biological maturation, adult men's negotiation of both potential milestones and unique challenges in the unfolding of their lives seemed less driven by a pre-wired epigenesis than by *adaptation*. Indeed, it now seemed presumptuous to impose as "normal" any set course of life on an array of different individuals. I concluded (1994, p. 208):

> Well-defined sequencing is probably not to be seen in a man's adult life. True, most men fall in love, marry, have children, work, see their children leave home, and retire before dying. But not every man undergoes this life progression. The priest, the exclusive homosexual, or the inveterate bachelor do not marry or have children. But while something may often be missing from their lives (children), they still feel like men. What is more, there is no lockstep timetable and course for an adult man's life. If an individual fails to fall in love at twenty-two, this does not necessarily preclude his doing so later on in midlife. Nor need one fall in love to marry or father a child. And while for most men a work identity is established before finding intimacy, this is not always the case—especially in instances of protracted schooling, long apprenticeships, and career changes.

In the spirit of the times, I had learned, as the cliché has it, how *little* I knew. Reflecting then and now, I wondered about the intellectual currents, socio-economic forces, and personal conflicts influencing my ideas about what it meant to be a man. Perhaps psychoanalysis' social critics were right, after all. Perhaps "masculinity" was really a construct in my own mind, as much as in those of the men I studied and treated, rather than an inherent fact of life. After all, when all was said and done, there was no such thing.

I have a picture from those Bellagio days. A half dozen resident scholars, all of them women, are aligned in a row, their cameras poised to snap simultaneously as they focus on the subject, a man (me), who is in turn photographing them.

Click! Not only feminism, but also postmodernism is in the air.

Back again and in conclusion: boys will be boys

A decade later, reviewing for the Committee on Women and

Psychoanalysis subject matter I left behind lest it and I become stale, I can set even such "perspectivalism", as Stolorow has termed it, in perspective. Slow to come to them, psychoanalysis has since become immersed in academia's gender studies, as well as in its more general postmodernist orientation to life. Faced with extinction, it has deconstructed itself.

In breaths of fresh air, old authoritarian presumptions have largely fallen away. Homosexuality has been depathologized, enabling clinicians of all sexual orientations to treat the lives of their gay patients, like those of the straight ones, as *real* lives—not "playing house", as one erstwhile supervisor of mine once put it. Indeed, masculinity and sexual orientation have been sorted out as separate vectors—a fact attested to in my own clinical work by the numbers of effeminate straight men and more virile gay males whom I happen to have treated (Ken Lewes has made this distinction). Feminized, the profession has become more feminist. The august *American Psychoanalytic* has admitted to it's precincts candidates from an array of disciplines. Indeed, as Michael Feldman recently noted, the Columbia Center—once so straight, male, and medical—may soon enough find that heterosexual male doctors are in the minority among its trainees and faculty.

But then again—how do we know we know anything? Certainly our patients want us to have a better lock on the truth about their history.

* * *

So do we have the *authority* to say anything about anything? Not in the stentorian voice of my callow youth, but rather in a murmur, I would answer, "Yes". Yes, boys will be boys whatever the "vicissitudes" (that old analytic catch-all) their life cycle holds in store for them. Just the other day a patient tells me of how fascinated his two-and-a-half-year-old son (the younger of the two) is with babies. Just the other night, a friend and physician comments on the videos of his daughter and of his son, the former serene and continuous in the movements and sounds it preserves, the latter a herky jerky and noisy record of hyperkinesis and high keyedness. Just today, a colleague tells me how much her little girl prefers her Barbies to the trucks that her parents have also given her. But then again—my little daughter's favourite toy just now is . . . a truck!

Yes, I think, boys will be boys; the boys I studied are still the boys I studied. And, yes, we psychoanalysts do indeed have something unique to say. However, only time will tell—time and empirical research.

Note

1. "Offending gender" by Martin Stephen Frommer was first published in the journal *Studies in Gender and Sexuality*, Vol. 1, pp. 191–206 published by Analytic Press. Reprinted with permission.

CHAPTER ELEVEN

Boy's envy of mother and the consequences of this narcissistic mortification[1]

Ruth F. Lax

F rom the many threads that form the matrix of male psychosexual development, this paper considers and examines only the narcissistic injury caused by the boy's realization that he will never attain mother's femaleness and procreative capacity. Although both boys and girls envy and covet mother's powerful bounty, there is a fundamental experiential difference between the sexes in that the girl can take comfort in her knowledge that, being like mother, she will mature to attain mother's female attributes. The boy, however, when he learns and acknowledges that he is different from mother, must recognize that his wish to attain mother's procreativity is doomed to fail. This fact evokes in him a painful narcissistic mortification that, usually inadequately repressed, may have lifelong consequences.

Introduction

Papers about men's envy of women, especially of women's procreative powers, are rare in the analytic literature. What papers there are have no follow-up or follow through—they are lost and forgotten. Boehm (1930), Jacobson (1950), Wisdom (1983), and Ross (1975), among others, attribute this paucity of adequate discussion to a resistance many analysts share that interferes with their recognition and acknowledgement of womb envy. This resistance is supported by the prevalent societal stereotypes.

Evidence of "womb envy" in adult males is frequently present when the wife is pregnant. "Womb envy" in males is not regarded as an aspect of their normative developmental process[2] and these vicissitudes are infrequently discussed.[3]

There is even greater resistance to the finding that the narcissistic pain of not being like mother and never being able to attain her procreative capacities is a significant factor contributing to a boy seeking identification with father, and the libidinal shift that results in father's becoming the primary love object for the boy. Although most analysts acknowledge and accept that the girl's narcissistic injury caused by not having a penis brings about her shift in libidinal object from mother to father, an analogous process in boys, stimulated by frustrated "womb envy" does not seem acceptable.[4]

I shall present vignettes to support my thesis.

Clinical vignettes

1. P. entered treatment after his girlfriend left him. This has been a shock to him because he had not known "anything was wrong". He thought "everything was fine". P, a very intellectual, obsessive man with an inordinate need for control, appeared quite shattered. He explained to me: "I did not suspect any trouble, how could I have been so blind? What did I miss? I could get over the fact that she left me, but I am horrified that I did not know she had decided to do so."

    P. was fully aware of his envy of women. It manifested itself in a tremendous rage toward them. The following are some remarks he made:

    "I envy women terribly ... with May I have one orgasm to her four. I can understand why primitive people perform clitoridectomies on women ... It is so unfair ... that men get to give women so much pleasure ... I can have only one orgasm and they have four. Nowadays ... women are considered to be the giving, generous, sensitive, mature ones, etc. and they say: 'Men should change to be more like women.' I remember, when I was a kid, we used to say: 'When will women be more like men?' I feel like raping them, no pleasure for them, just for me. It would show them, just bang them about."

P. became enraged and depressed when he found out that his sister-in-law was pregnant. He recalled feelings evoked by his mother's pregnancy. P. was five at the time. He remembered saying to his mother, "How could you do this without asking me? I don't want a baby and I don't want you to have a baby either." He recalled wanting to hit his mother on the stomach to make the baby "fall out so he could get rid of it". After a long silence, P. said: "I must confess, when I see a pregnant woman I still would like to punch her in the stomach and pull the baby out. Women should not have babies. They do not know what to do with them. It should be the right of the man ... (long silence). I should have a baby. My brother's wife is a stupid goose."

P's "womb envy" was quite conscious and fuelled his rage at women. P. reinforced the denial of the feminine aspects of his character by machismo bravura and hostile enactments in relation to women. Simultaneously, however, the nurturing, loving, and empathetic aspects of his self, the so-called feminine aspects, manifested themselves in his treatment of his pets and in his care for the handicapped child of a friend.

2. F., a psychiatric resident who was also a candidate in an analytic institute, came for treatment "because that was one of the requirements for becoming an analyst". He reported having few symptoms other than occasional anxiety feelings, occurring mostly in situations where he would be in some "performing role" and feared he would "not do as well as he wished". He also occasionally felt depressed when he did not have a sense of being admired. F. had married a woman who pursued, courted, and admired him greatly. He did not think much of her, but greatly enjoyed her admiration. Their relationship was good since she did what he wanted most: she adored him.

    The harmony of their relationship was disrupted when his wife became pregnant three months after F. started his analysis. F. at that time began to complain that she was stupid, did not take proper care of herself, and did things that would result in a miscarriage so that "he would lose his baby".

When his wife began to "show", F., who until then had a rather athletic build, began to gain weight and developed a paunch. It seemed to me that his gait changed and that his movements were sluggish.

At the end of his wife's fifth month of pregnancy, F. began to complain about peculiar feelings in his abdomen and increased constipation. He did not know whether these were "gas pains or some sort of spasms". Over the next few weeks his physical complaints filled most of his analytic time. He reported that his symptoms were increasing and was preoccupied with "these vague sensations and pains". He became quite hypochondriacal, worrying that he might have some malignancy. F. finally saw a physician who could not find "anything wrong", prescribed some laxative, and suggested "more exercise". F. ignored these recommendations and experienced no relief. Within the next six weeks he consulted two more physicians and had a GI series and a colonoscopy. The results of these procedures were negative. F. insisted his pains "got worse" and he became more and more preoccupied with himself. His wife at that time was beginning the seventh month. F. in a state of extreme hypochondria, was complaining all the time of great discomfort. He decided to take a medical leave of absence from his residency and interrupted his analytic training.

The material in the sessions was filled with concerns that he had a "rapidly growing malignant tumour". F. resisted any interpretations in which I attempted to show a connection between his physical complaints and fears and his wife's pregnancy. He accused me of lack of compassion and empathy and of being a feminist and siding with his wife. His negative transference was overpowering.

During the eighth month of pregnancy, F. found a surgeon who agreed to perform an exploratory abdominal operation. At this time he had absolutely no insight, and analytic work was impossible. He was totally preoccupied with the impending operation and interrupted his analysis.

Three months after a baby girl was born, F.'s wife phoned me and insisted on seeing me "since I knew F". She was in great despair. She reported that the results of F's operation were negative. After the birth of the baby, F. took over almost completely the care of the infant. He maintained that she was "an inadequate mother" because she could not nurse, and that he "had better qualifications to care for the baby" than she. F. threatened to leave her and take the baby away if she did not comply. She said, "He urged me to have a baby: he behaves as if it was he who had the baby, as if I had no part in it, not even giving birth to it. I feel shoved aside like an emptied vessel."

During the time he was in analysis, F. did not report any conscious pregnancy or birthing fantasies. However, his behaviour since his wife became pregnant indicates the presence of a strong unconscious wish to be pregnant, to birth and to mother. This wish appears to have been so deeply repressed that it could only be enacted.[5]

3. Dr B., a chemist, came into treatment because of potency problems. He was a high-functioning man with a narcissistic character who derived great satisfaction from his work. The following process notes from analytic sessions depict his attitudes toward women and his envy of them.

> There is some funny confusion about wanting to be a beautiful woman and being a beautiful woman. When I masturbate, I masturbate face down as if I were ashamed. I like the idea of telling a woman what to wear and how to make-up. It is like controlling and restraining a woman. This brings to mind deformation and mutilation. I envy women's tits so I want to punish them, to mutilate them—I was thinking there were times when I was very effeminate as I was growing up. The real fantasy is I should be a woman some of the time and a man at other times. Debbie told me she would like to have a machine she could get into and change her appearance. I would like to be a woman who would have that kind of machine.

> One of the inside excuses for not going to bed with a woman is that it does not get me any closer to being a woman. With Debbie I can identify vicariously, whereas Tina, whom I love, does not excite me. She is more like the kind of man I would like to be. I want a woman who is like I wanted to be.

> I have been thinking: physiologically there is not much difference between the sexes: just one of the twenty-three chromosomes is different. Just the mammary glands and the genitals are different. I trivialize the differences. When I look at Tina she is like the man I would like to be.

Now with Debbie the differences are great, but I don't sleep with her either. Debbie reads girls' magazines. I would like to read them too. I trivialize Debbie by saying she is a silly little girl.

To go after something, someone, is to admit you are in need—that you want comforting—and that is something I could never do because only flaky people and weak people need comforting.

RL: Women?

I really don't expect much from a mate. I want comforting, which I never got from Mom, and I want my mate to be seductive and sexy and tempting and she has to be intelligent and impressive to my parents and my grandparents. She has to fulfil the requirements of the gene pool.

Several months later, speaking about his mother and the birth of his younger brother, Dr B. said, "A woman can do everything I do, but I can't do what she does ... have babies."

Several years into his analysis Dr B. said: "Which type of woman a man ultimately chooses depends on what he would have liked to be—and therefore with whom he can and would rather vicariously identify. I still can't make up my mind."

Toward the end of his analysis, Dr B. fell in love with a brilliant student in his field, eight years his junior, whose mentor he became. Jane was grateful for Dr B's help with her scientific work. She also permitted him to pick her clothes, "dress her up", "do" her fingernails and toenails, decide on her hairdo, and choose her jewellery. Dr B. was happy. He said, "When I dress her I feel as if I'm dressing myself. All the things I wanted to wear Jane wears. It is beautiful. When we make love it is as if I caress a part of me. I get excited and we have sex. Good sex. I feel very gratified.

*   *   *

Mother, because of her affective and caring relationship with her offspring becomes the first love object for infants of either sex. The gratifying nurturing experiences of the oral phase account for an identification with mother that is associated simultaneously with her body and with the cessation of hunger, providing a sense of internal physical satiation and fulfilment. Mother is thus experienced as the provider, bountiful, powerful, seen as omnipotent, who in the child's fantasy can make everything it wants happen. The child identifies with a mother experienced as active and producing.

Usually, as the toddler grows, this loving, blissful relationship with mother becomes interspersed with frustration and conflict. Mother is perceived as "good" when the child feels gratified, as "bad" when what the child wants is not forthcoming. Envy, rage, fear, and shame are aroused by the toddler's relative helplessness and dependency on the mother, experienced as all-powerful, although frequently ungratifying. Consequently, what the child wants is not always forthcoming. What the child wants is to actively dominate, love, and punish mother—it wants to be in mother's place. Toddlers of both sexes tell their mothers they want to grow up fast and become mum; then, mum will be the baby. Mothers who understand and agree to play the game in which the roles are reversed find that their children can be most cruel, punishing, and restrictive, experiencing in this game, as well as in games with dolls and animals, how they experience the overwhelming power of the mother. The mother–baby game also expresses the child's enormous wish to usurp all of mother's powers and attributes especially her capacity to procreate, her most coveted attribute (Ross, 1975, 1977).

Children's oral and anal fantasies of how "babies are made" and how babies are birthed are familiar. Pregnancy fantasies in boys and girls precede the so-called phallic phase (Brunswick, 1940; Klein, 1921). Jacobson states: "The wish for a baby precedes the wish for a penis in girls and the pride in the penis in boys" (1950, p. 141). During this phase the child wants both to get a baby from mother and to give one to her. There is no understanding of father's role. In fantasy, the wish to make a baby is equally strong in boys and girls and finds fulfilment in their fantasies (Ross, 1977, pp. 331–334).

By two-and-a-half-years toddlers become aware of anatomic differences. In the following year core gender identity consolidates, resulting in increased awareness of the genitals (Tyson & Tyson, 1990). Usually at this time children of each sex begin to show differences in the nature and content of their envy of mother's attributes and procreative powers.

Brunswick, in "The pre-oedipal phase" (1940),[6] states that the wish for a baby in young boys stems from their normal and phase-specific identification with the active mother (p. 309) who can make babies and give birth to them.[7] The boy envies mother's breasts not only because they are big, bigger than his penis, but specifically because they have milk and mother can suckle a babe. With maturation, however, the envious boy becomes more and more aware of the fact that he is not like mother. Boys, unlike girls, cannot take comfort in the future, since they know they will never grow up to give birth to babies and to nurse them. This immutable fact is most difficult for boys to accept. It is painful, enraging, and deeply upsetting.

While a boy is struggling with his wish to be like mother and identify with her, he is simultaneously enraged with her for having made him different from her. The boy at this time is also becoming more and more consciously aware of his penis, which is his source of pleasure (as the girl's genitals are hers). The confrontation between the reality of his gender and the inordinately strong wish for mother's powers results in a period of great psychic turbulence for a boy.

As a boy recognizes that his wish to be like mother is doomed to failure, he appears to suffer greatly from a sense of inferiority, since at this stage he considers mother's endowment superior to men's (Boehm, 1930; Klein, 1921). A sense of intense narcissistic mortification may follow. However, the boy's painful recognition of his differences from mother will eventually become the significant impetus for his turning to father as his primary love object. The boy will, at this time, seek his father, who is, like his son, endowed with a penis. He will be prompted to consolidate his early identifications with father and will fantasize about father's powers.

Having become aware of anatomic differences, the boy knows that he has a penis and eventually, that his all-powerful mother does not. At first, however, he consistently denies this knowledge about mother. The denial is motivated both by the childish belief "that everyone must be like me" (Freud, 1905), and also by the powerful wish that he and mother be alike. The boy thus "endows" his mother with a penis. This is a projection of his body image onto her. At this stage of development making mother phallic[8]1 undoes the narcissistic hurt of not being like mother. Thus, the fantasy of a phallic mother is at first a defensive transitional fantasy helpful to a boy who is struggling with the narcissistic pain of not having mother's powers. The subsequent narcissistic over-investment in the power of the erect penis—which is not the same as sexual enjoyment of the erect penis—compensates a boy for the narcissistic injury of being different from mother.

To give up the wish of pregnancy, child bearing, and suckling is difficult for the boy. The child's fantasy that mother is omnipotent and possesses the power to fulfil his wishes, to inflict and to ward off pain and evil, increases the boy's rage at mother for not having endowed him with her attributes and for having instead given them to the girl.

Since renunciation of these overwhelming feelings is usually almost impossible, and since the boy is also unable to tolerate the narcissistic pain and mortification they evoke, repression sets in. Men's dreams and fantasies reveal that such repression is never totally successful, and that the wishes persist forever in men's unconscious (e.g. Boehm, 1930; Jacobson, 1950). To prevent "seepage", due to inadequate repression, bolstering by additional defence mechanisms is necessary. This is usually accomplished by various reaction formations. Sublimations that allow for creativity— model building, art, etc.—and the fulfilment of nurturing wishes by raising pets, gardening, and the like lead, when present, to healthy resolutions.

Greenson (1966, p. 68) maintains that a boy can establish a real masculine gender identity only if he *dis-identifies* with his mother. Thus, to counteract the persistent unconscious wish for sameness and identification with mother, the boy at this time actively seeks his father and vigorously attempts to be like him. The boy wants a father to adore and to emulate, a father who is strong and powerful, a father who will substitute and compensate for the enforced loss of mother. He wants a father to be the model to which he can aspire (Ross, 1985/1986; Tyson & Tyson, 1990).

To become masculine, a boy must sense that his father likes being a man and enjoys his male attributes. The boy's wish to emulate his father is initially defensive stemming from his repressed maternal identification. Greenson maintains that to achieve a dis-identification from mother, a boy must "use the father to form not only a counter but a contra-identification to the mother"[9] (1968, p. 373). The boy consciously strives to be like father and feel united with him, bonded in a sense of "us men" (Tyson & Tyson, 1990).

Analysis reveals that the stronger the boy's unconscious envy of mother, the more uncertain his sense of masculinity and the louder his proclamations of manliness. By latency these defensive reaction formations usually manifest themselves in a fully developed disparaging attitude toward girls and women. Conscious repudiation, disgust as well as antagonism, and distaste for everything feminine are accentuated. Any so-called feminine attributes are vehemently denied. To be a boy means to be hard, tough, rough, and belligerent, to take chances and disparage women's pursuits. Our society helps the boy deny his feminine yearning by supporting and cultivating his aggression and sadism, expressed in many competitive games and sports, and also by partially channelling these impulses toward girls and women.

Discussion and conclusions

Jacobson (1950) attributes the meagre discussion of men's "woman-envy" to the repression in men of wishes for feminine attributes, subsequently reinforced by reaction formations. Insufficient analysis of such defences and of repressed wishes in training analysts could lead to a constriction and possible scotoma for derivatives of "woman-envy" wishes in their male patients. This may result in a perpetuation in men of analyses that do not reach the earliest stages of the mother–infant–toddler relationship occurring during the pregenital phase. Zilboorg (1944) maintained that androcentric bias kept even psychoanalysts from recognizing the extent of femininity in spite of their masculine attributes. The extent of men's repression of "woman-envy" can be surmised from the discomfort a man experiences at any hint of femininity in his make-up.

The need for acceptance of the inevitable difference from mother occurs at a time when the boy's psyche has few resources that could encompass such a loss. He therefore feels bereft, and disadvantaged. Since our society devalues women a boy is not helped to work through his loss and mourn it. His envy of mother's attributes are forcefully, though inadequately, repressed. The boy is helped in the repression of his feminine longing by reaction formations based on the stereotypes of masculinity enforced by society and the general patriarchal bias.

Betcher and Pollack (1993) regard the societally enforced separation of the boy from the loving, nurturing mother–son interaction as the bedrock of the "male-wound" and as a traumatic premature object loss. My observations indicate that this separation, which is traumatic, follows an even greater trauma: the narcissistic wound that the boy experiences when he realizes he is not the same as mother. This is the time when a boy seeks out the available father. The ease and speed of such a transition may further contribute to the repression, not only of envy of maternal attributes, but also of longing for maternal loving nurturance. A hasty repression also contributes to the erection of reaction formation to maintain the repressed.

It is possible, and even likely, that the process of father-seeking by a boy and the enforced separation from the mother-orbit coincide, or at least reinforce, each other. A patriarchal culture, which imposes on the boy codes of manliness that are highly valued, exacerbates the need for this separation. It lauds strict autonomy, denies relational needs, and emphasizes valour. These are frequently manifested in a disregard of one's own emotional needs and the needs of others.

Repression of woman-envy leads to many pathological outcomes, such as disturbances in gender identity, sexual inhibitions, the inability to attain genuine sex-relatedness, and certain forms of homosexuality, transvestitism, and transsexualism (Fierstein, 1988). Most important in such cases, however, is the frequency of narcissistic object choices. A man, in this case, chooses a woman he would like to be or wanted to be in the past, each choice providing a narcissistic fulfilment. Such choices, however, preclude the possibility of object love. Jacobson (1937/1976), discussing male and female narcissism and its vicissitudes, stated that in the woman narcissism merges into object love, whereas in the male it takes precedence over object love (p. 535).

Of even greater significance than the suffering of the individual is the cost to society. Psychic conflicts stemming from repressed "woman-envy" and the enforced separation from mother, deemed necessary to attain masculinity, may manifest themselves in defensive sexism combined with notions of conquest, violence, self-display, and machismo. All these stem from the close relationship between envy and the devaluation of women (Boehm, 1930; Kernberg, 1974; Zilboorg, 1944), which must be explored in order to understand defensive masculinity.

Notes

1. A longer, more encompassing version of this paper, including mythological, anthropologic and religious material, was published in *The Psychoanalytic Study of the Child*, Vol. 52, 1997.

2. The term "normative" is used as Freud used it when he discussed the oedipal development in boys and penis envy in girls. In these discussions Freud did not consider *a priori* criteria against which normality of development is measured. Rather, Freud, mainly on the basis of reconstructions from adult analyses, self-analysis, and possibly some child observation, arrived at a model of psychosexual development for boys and girls. Though Freud knew of "womb envy" (1909b, 1918b), he did not include this fact in his descriptions of a boy's developmental progression.

3. One of the exceptions is the analysis of Rilke's poetry by Simenauer (1954).

4. Papers by Greenson (1952, 1968) and Stoller and Herdt (1982) that discuss the boy's process of "disidentification from mother" have also not been sufficiently examined, although they are often quoted. These authors maintain that unless a boy disidentifies from mother he will be feminized and that father's active presence is necessary to bring about disidentification from mother.

5. Evans (1951) discusses the effect of pregnancy which led to a breakdown in a male.

6. Supposedly written with Freud.

7. Bettelheim, 1954; Boehm, 1930; Brunswick, 1940; Eisler, 1921; Evans, 1951; Fierstein, 1988; Freud, 1909b, 1918b, 1925; Herdt, 1981; Jacobson, 1950; Jaffe, 1966; Roheim, 1942; Ross, 1975, 1977; Stoller and Herdt, 1982; Tyson and Tyson, 1990, amongst others.

8. I am aware that it is usually assumed that a boy denies the existence of anatomic differences out of castration anxiety. In my opinion, this motivation occurs later, during the oedipal phase, as a reaction to the fantasied threats by the father to squelch the boy's incestuous desires and rebellious impetus. Thus, the phallic mother is, at first, a defensive fantasy motivated by a wish for sameness with mother. The phallic woman, used pejoratively, develops after a boy represses his wish for sameness with the mother. It is a derivative of the wish in each male to repudiate the feminine within him; this usually occurs simultaneously with an overvaluation of the penis (Brunswick, 1940; Jacobson, 1950).

9. This position is maintained by Stoller and Herdt (1982) with even greater emphasis.

REFERENCES

Alizade, A. M. (1991). El naufragio (Untergang). Del complejo de Edipo en la mujer. In: Alizade (Ed.), *Voces de Feminidad*. Buenos Aires.

Alizade, A. M. (1992a). Las series ecuacionales simbólicas en el devenir de una mujer. Paper read at the Symposium of the Argentine Psychoanalytic Association, Buenos Aires, October, 1992.

Alizade, A. M. (1992b). *Feminine Sensuality*. London: Karnac Books, 1999.

Amati Mehler, J. (1992). Love and male impotence. *International Journal Psycho-Analysis*, 73: 467.

Anzieu, A. (1987). La envoltura de excitación. In: *Las Envolturas Psíquicas*. Buenos Aires: Amorrortu Editores, 1990.

Anzieu, D. (1985). *Le Moi Peau*. Paris: Dunod.

Argentieri, S. (1990). Il sesso degli angeli. In: *Del Genere Sessuale*. Roma: Borla.

Assoun, P.-L. (1989). *El Perverso y la Mujer en la Literatura*. Buenos Aires: Nueva Visión, 1995.

Basaglia, F. (1984). La mujer y la locura. In: S. Marcos (Ed.), *Antipsiquiatría y Política* (pp. 150–171). Mexico City: Ed. Extemporáneos.

Baudelot, C., & Establet, R. (1992). *Allez les Filles!* Paris: Seuil.

Benjamin, J. (1988). *The Bonds of Love*. New York: Pantheon.

Betcher, W., & Pollack, W. (1993). *In a Time of Fallen Heroes. The Recreation of Masculinity*. New York: Atheneum (Macmillan).

137

Bettleheim, B. (1954). *Symbolic Wounds*. New York: Free Press of Glencoe.

Bibring, G. L. (1940). On an oral component in masculine inversion. *Internationale Zeitschrift für Psychoanalyse, 24*: 29–38.

Bion, W. R. (1965). *Transformations*. Heinemann Medical [reprinted London: Karnac Books, 1984].

Bion, W. R. (1967). *Second Thoughts*. Heinemann Medical [reprinted London: Karnac Books, 1984].

Bion, W. R. (1970). *Attention and Interpretation*. London: Tavistock Publications [reprinted London: Karnac Books, 1984].

Bion, W. R. (1975). *A Memoir of the Future, Book One: The Dream*. Rio de Janeiro, Brazil: Imago Editora.

Bion, W. R. (1977). *A Memoir of the Future, Book Two: The Past Presented*. Rio de Janeiro, Brazil: Imago Editora.

Bion, W. R. (1977). *Two Papers: The Grid and the Caesura*. Rio de Janiero, Brazil: Imago Editora.

Bion, W. R. (1979). *A Memoir of the Future, Book Three: The Dawn of Oblivion*. Strathclyde: Clunie Press.

Bleger, J. (1967). *Simbiosis y Ambiguedad*. Buenos Aires: Ed. Paidós.

Blos, P. (1962). *On Adolescence: A Psychoanalytic Interpretation*. New York: Free Press.

Blum, A., & Pfetzing, V. (1997). Assaults to the self: The trauma of growing up gay. *Gender & Psychoanalysis, 2*: 427–442.

Boehm, F. (1930). The femininity-complex in men. *International Journal Psycho-Analysis, 11*: 444–469.

Bonino, L. (1989). Mortalidad en la adolescencia y estereotipos masculinos, Jornadas de Atención Primaria de la Salud, Buenos Aires (mimeographed).

Borch-Jacobsen, M. (1988). *The Freudian Subject*. Stanford, CA: Stanford University Press.

Brunswick, M. R. (1940). The pre-oedipal phase of the libido development. *Psychoanalytic Quarterly, 9*: 292–319.

Butler, J. (1995). Melancholy gender—refused identification. *Psychoanalytical Dialogue, 5*: 165–180.

Butler, J. (1998). Analysis to the core: commentary on papers by J. Hansell and D. Elise. *Psychoanalytical Dialogue, 8*: 373–378.

Castoriadis-Aulagnier, P. (1975). *La Violencia de la Interpretación*. Buenos Aires: Amorrortu, 1977.

Castro, R., & Bronfman, M. (1993). Teoría feminista y sociología médica: bases para una discusión. *Cadernos de Saúde Pública, 9*(3): 375–394.

Chasseguet-Smirgel, J. (1985). *Creativity and Perversion*. London: Free Association Books.

Chiland, C. (1997). *Changer de Sexe*. Paris: Odile Jacob.

Chodorow, N. (1978). *The Reproduction of Mothering*. Berkeley, University of California Press.

Chodorow, N. (1992). Heterosexuality as a compromise formation: reflections on the psychoanalytic theory of sexual development. *Psychoanalysis and Contemporary Thought, 15*: 267–304.

Colette, S. (1927). La vagabonde. In: Gallimard (Ed.), *Bibliothèque de la Pléiade*, Vol. 1, 1984.

Corbett, K. (1996). Homosexual boyhood: notes on girlyboys. *Gender & Psychoanalysis, 1*: 429–462.

Davis, K., & Blake, J. (1956). Social structure and fertility: an analytic framework. *Economic Development and Cultural Change, 4*: 211–235.

De Keijzer, B. (1995). Masculinity as a risk factor. Seminar on Fertility and the Male Life Cycle in the Era of Fertility Decline, Zacatecas, Mexico (mimeographed).

Dimen, M. (1991). Deconstructing difference: gender splitting and transitional space. *Psychoanalytical Dialogue, 1*: 335–352.

Drescher, J. (1998). *Psychoanalytic Therapy and the Gay Man*. Hillsdale, NJ: The Analytic Press.

Eisler, M. J. (1921). A man's unconscious fantasy of pregnancy in the guise of traumatic hysteria. *International Journal of Psycho-Analysis, 2*: 253–296.

Evans, W. (1951). Simulated pregnancy in a male. *Psychoanalysis, 20*: 165–178.

Fairbairn, W. R. D. (1944). Endopsychic structure considered in terms of object relations. In: *Psychoanalytic Studies of Personality*. New York: Routledge, 1952.

Faure-Oppenheimer, A. (1980). *La Elección de Sexo*. Madrid: Akal, 1986.

Ferenczi, S. (1923). *Thalassa. A Theory of Genitality*. New York: The Psychoanalytic Quarterly, 1938.

Fierstein, H. (1988). *Torch Song Trilogy*. New York: New American Library, A Signet Book.

Figueroa, J. (1998). Algunos elementos para interpretar la presencia de los varones en los procesos de salud reproductiva. *Cadernos de Saúde Pública, 14*(1): 87–96.

Freud, A. (1952). A connection between the states of negativism and of emotional surrender (Horigkeit). *International Journal Psycho-Analysis, 33*: 265.

Freud, A. (1965). Normality and pathology in childhood. In: *The Writings of Anna Freud, Volume 6.*

Freud, S. (1897). Draft M. In: James Strachey (Ed.), *The Standard Edition of the Complete Psychological Works of Sigmund Freud, Volume 1 (S.E., 1).* London: Hogarth Press.

Freud, S. (1905). Three essays on the theory of sexuality. *S.E., 7.*

Freud, S. (1908a). On the sexual theories of children. *S.E., 9.*

Freud, S. (1908b). "Civilized" sexual morality and modern nervous illness. *S.E., 9.*

Freud, S. (1909a). Analysis of a five year old boy. *S.E., 10.*

Freud, S. (1909b). Analysis of a phobia in a five year old. *S.E., 10*: 3–149.

Freud, S. (1910a). A special type of object choice made by men. *S.E., 11.*

Freud, S. (1910b). Leonardo da Vinci and a memory of his childhood. *S.E., 11*: 63–137.

Freud, S. (1910c). Letter to Dr Friedrich S. Krauss on Anthropophyteia. *S.E., 11.*

Freud, S. (1910–1912). Contributions to the psychology of love, I and II. *S.E., 11.*

Freud, S. (1912). On the universal tendency to debasement in the sphere of love. *S.E., 11.*

Freud, S. (1913). *Totem and Taboo. S.E., 13.*

Freud, S. (1914). On narcissism: an introduction. *S.E., 14.*

Freud, S. (1915). The unconscious. *S.E., 14.*

Freud, S. (1916). *Introductory Lectures on Psychoanalysis. S.E., 15, 16.*

Freud, S. (1918a). Contributions to the psychology of love, III: The taboo of virginity. *S.E., 17*: 191–208.

Freud, S. (1918b). From the history of an infantile neurosis. *S.E., 17*: 3–122.

Freud, S. (1920a). The psychogenesis of a case of homosexuality in a woman. *S.E., 18.*

Freud, S. (1920b). *Beyond the Pleasure Principle. S.E., 18.*

Freud, S. (1923a). Neurosis and psicosis. *S.E., 19.*

Freud, S. (1923b). *The Ego and the Id. S.E., 19.*

Freud, S. (1924a). The dissolution of the Oedipus complex. *S.E., 19*: 173–179.

Freud, S. (1924b). The economic problem of masochism. *S.E., 19.*

Freud, S. (1925). Some psychical consequences of the anatomical distinction between the sexes. *S.E., 19*: 243–258.

Freud, S. (1926a). *Inhibitions, Symtoms and Anxiety. S.E., 20.*

Freud, S. (1926b). The question of lay analysis. *S.E., 20.*

Freud, S. (1927). Fetishim. *S.E., 21.*

Freud, S. (1930). *Civilization and its Discontents. S.E., 21.*

Freud, S. (1931b). Female sexuality. *S.E., 21*: 223.

Freud, S. (1933a). Femininity. *S.E., 22*: 112.

Freud, S. (1937). *Analysis Terminable and Interminable. S.E., 23.*

Freud, S. (1938a). An outline of psychoanalysis. *S.E., 23.*

Freud, S. (1938b). Splitting of the ego in the process of defence. *S.E., 23.*

Friedman, R. (1988). *Male Homosexuality: A Contemporary Psychoanalytic Perspective.* New Haven, CT: Yale University Press.

Frommer, M. S. (1994). Homosexuality and psychoanalysis: technical considerations revisited. *Psychoanalytical Dialogue, 4*: 215–233.

Frommer, M. S. (1995). Countertransference obscurity in the psychoanalytic treatment of homosexual patients. In: T. Domenici & R. Lesser (Eds.), *Disorienting Sexuality.* New York: Routledge.

García, C. (n.d.). *Actitudes, opiniones y representaciones sociales del aborto y la contracepción en hombres.* Ministerio de Salud Pública, Havana, Cuba (mimeographed).

Gilligan, C. (1982). *In a Different Voice: Psychological Theory and Women's Moral Development.* Cambridge: Harvard University Press.

Giménez de Vainer, A., & Glocer Fiorini, L. (1995). Transexualismo: entre el mito y la ciencia. *Revista de Psicoanalisis, 52*(1): 107–118.

Glocer Fiorini, L. (1998). The feminine in psychoanalysis. A complex construction. *Journal of Clinical Psychoanalysis, 7*: 421–439.

Glocer Fiorini, L. (2001). *Lo Femenino y el Pensamiento Complejo.* Buenos Aires: Lugar Editorial.

Goldner, V. (1991). Toward a critical relational theory of gender. *Psychoanalytical Dialogue, 1*: 249–272.

Goy, R. W., Berkovitch, F. B., & McBrair, M. C. (1988). Behavioral masculinization is independent of genital masculinization in prenatally androgenized female rhesus macaques. *Hormones and Behavior, 22*: 552–571.

Green, A. (1990). *La Nueva Clínica Psicoanalítica y la Teoría Freudiana.* Buenos Aires: Amorrortu Editores.

Green, A. (1999). *The Work of the Negative.* London: Free Association Books.

Green, A. (2001). *Life Narcissism Death Narcissism.* London: Free Association Books.

Greene, M., & Biddlecom, A. (2000). Absent and problematic men: demographic accounts of male reproductive roles. *Population and Development Review, 26*(1): 81–115.

Greenson, R. (1952). The struggle against identification. In: *Explorations in Psychoanalysis.* New York: International Universities Press.

Greenson, R. (1966). A transvestite boy and a hypothesis. *International Journal of Psycho-Analysis*, 47: 396.

Greenson, R. (1968). Dis-identifying from mother: its special importance for the boy. *International Journal of Psycho-Analysis*, 49: 370.

Hansell, J. (1998). Gender anxiety, gender melancholia, gender perversion. *Psychoanalytical Dialogue*, 8: 337–352.

Harris, A. (1991). Gender as contradiction. *Psychoanalytical Dialogue*, 1: 197–224.

Hausman, B. L. (1995). *Changing Sex: Transsexualism, Technology, and the Idea of Gender*. Durham, NC: Duke University Press.

Herdt, G. (1981). *Guardians of the Flutes: Idioms of Masculinity*. McGraw Hill.

Herdt, G. (Ed.) (1994). *Third Sex, Third Gender, Beyond Sexual Dimorphism in Culture and History*. New York: Zone Books.

Hernández, J. (1995). Sexualidad masculina y reproducción. ¿Qué va a decir papá?, Latin American Colloquium on "Males, Sexuality, and Reproduction", Zacatecas, Mexico (mimeographed).

Hierro, G. (1990). La doble moral burguesa mexicana vs. la nueva moral de la igualdad. In: J. Ramírez (Ed.), *Normas y Prácticas Morales y Cívicas en la Vida Cotidiana* (pp. 185–216). Mexico: National Autonomous University of Mexico.

Jacobson, E. (1937/1976). Ways of female superego formation and the female castration conflict. *Psychoanalytic Quarterly*, 45: 525–538.

Jacobson, E. (1950). Development of the wish for a child in boys. *Psychoanalytic Study of the Child*, 5: 139–152.

Jaffe, D. S. (1966). The masculine envy of women's procreative function. *Journal of the American Psychoanalytic Association*, 16: 621–648.

Kakar, S., & Ross, J. (1987). *Tales of Love, Sex and Danger*. New York: Basil Blackwell.

Kaplan, L. (1991). *Perversiones Femeninas. Las Tentaciones de Emma Bovary*. Buenos Aires: Paidós, 1994.

Kernberg, O. (1974a). Barriers to falling and remaining in love. *Journal of the American Psychoanalytic Association*, 22: 486–514.

Kernberg, O. (1974b). Mature love, prerequisites and characteristics. *Journal of the American Psychoanalytic Association*, 22: 743–768.

Kernberg, O. (1977). Boundaries and structures in love relations. *Journal of the American Psychoanalytic Association*, 25: 81–116.

Kernberg, O. (1980). *The Internal World and External Reality*. New York: Aronson.

Klein, M. (1921). The development of a child. In: *Contributions to Psychoanalysis* (pp. 13–67). London: Hogarth Press, 1948.

Klein, M. (1932). *The Psychoanalysis of Children*. London: Hogarth Press.

Klein, M. (1946). Notes on some schizoid mechanisms. In: *Envy and Gratitude and Other Works, Volume 3*. London: Hogarth Press.

Klein, M. (1957). *Envidia y Gratitud*, Vol. 6. Buenos Aires: Paidós, O.C.

Koestenbaum, W. (1993). *The Queen's Throat: Opera, Homosexuality and the Mystery of Desire*. New York: Poseidon Press.

Kohut, H. (1971). *Análisis del Self*. Buenos Aires: Amorrortu Editores.

Lacan, J. (1958). La signification du phallus. In: *Écrits*. Paris: Seuil, 1966.

Lagarde, M. (1994). La regulación social del género: El género como filtro de poder. In: *Enciclopedia de la Sexualidad* (pp. 389–425). Mexico: Consejo Nacional de Población.

Lamas, M. (1993). La bioética: proceso social y cambio de valores. *Sociológica*, 8(22): 187–203.

Laplanche, J. (1980). *Castración. Simbolizaciones: Problemáticas II*. Buenos Aires: Amorrortu Editores, 1988.

Layton, L. (1998). *Who's that Girl? Who's that Boy? Clinical Practice Meets Postmodern Gender Theory*. Northvale, NJ: Aronson.

Leal, O., & Fachel, J. (1995). Male reproductive culture and sexuality in South Brazil: combining ethnographic data and statistical analysis. Seminar on Fertility and the Male Life Cycle in the Era of Fertility Decline, Zacatecas, Mexico (mimeographed).

Liberman, D. (1970). *Lingüística—Interacción Comunicativa y Proceso Psicoanalítico*. Buenos Aires: Nueva Visión.

Liberman y Maldavsky, D. (1975). *Psicoanálisis y Semiótica*. Buenos Aires: Paidós.

Lutenberg, J. (1992). Transferencia y verdad. *Rev. Psic. de APdeBA*, 14(1), Buenos Aires.

Lutenberg, J. (1993). El vínculo transferencial—Reedición edición. *Revista de psicoanálisis de Madrid*, 18, November 1993.

Lutenberg, J. (1994). Sobreadaptación, duelos impensables y superyo. *Revista. Actualidad Psicológica*, No. 208, Buenos Aires.

Lutenberg, J. (1995a). Clínica del vacío. El vacío mental y la angustia. Reflexiones clínicas y técnicas acerca del acting. *Rev. Zona Erógena*, No. 26, Buenos Aires.

Lutenberg, J. (1995b). Las simbiosis defensivas y las identificaciones estructurances. *Revista*.

Maccoby, E. E. (1988). Gender as a social category. *Developmental Psychology*, 24(6): 755–765 [reprinted in *Annual Progress in Child Psychiatry and Child Development*, 1989, pp. 127–150].

Maccoby, E. E. (1990). Gender and relationships, a developmental account. *American Psychologist, 45*(4) April: 513–520.

Madrid, M. (1993). La alternativa crítica de Carol Gilligan. In: *Perspectivas Feministas* (anthology) (pp. 55–63). Mexico: Benemérita Universidad Autónoma de Puebla.

Mahler, M. (1967). *On Human Symbiosis and the Vicissitudes on Individuation. Selected Papers.* New York: Aronson.

Mahler, M. (1984). *Separación Individuación.* Buenos Aires: Ed. Piados.

McDougall, J. (1989). *Theaters of the Body.* New York & London: W. W. Norton.

Meltzer, D. (1973). *Sexual States of Mind.* Perthshire, Scotland: Clunie Press.

Millot, C. (1983). *Exsexo. Ensayo Sobre el Transexualismo.* Buenos Aires: Catálogos.

Morin, E. (1990). *Introducción al Pensamiento Complejo.* Barcelona: Gedisa, 1995.

Mundigo, A., & Indriso, C. (1999). *Abortion in the Developing World.* New Delhi, India: Vistaar Publications.

Nasio, J. D. (1990). La femineidad del padre. In: A. M. Alizade (Ed. & Pub.), *Voces de Femineidad.* Buenos Aires. 1991.

Nunberg, H. (1938). Homosexuality, magic and aggression. *International Journal of Psycho-Analysis, 19*: 1–16.

Núñez, L., & Palma, Y. (1991). El aborto en México. *FEM: Publicación Feminista Mensual, 15*(104): 4–15.

Potter, J. (1982). El uso de variables intermedias para la evaluación de los datos de fecundidad reciente. In: *Investigación Demográfica en México, 1980* (pp. 81–91). Mexico City: National Council on Science and Technology.

Quinodoz, D. (1998). A fe/male transsexual patient in psychoanalysis, *International Journal of Psycho-Analysis, 79*(1): 95–111.

Roheim, G. (1930). *Psychoanalysis and Anthropology.* New York: International Universities Press.

Roheim, G. (1942). Transition rites. *Psychoanalytic Quarterly, 11*: 336–374.

Roiphe, H., & Galenson, E. (1981). *Infantile Origins of Sexual Identity.* New York: International Universities Press.

Rosenfeld, H. (1965). *Psychotic States.* New York: International Universities Press.

Ross, J. (1975). The development of paternal identity: a critical review of the literature on nurturance and generativity in boys and men. *Journal of the American Psychoanalytic Association, 23*: 783–817.

Ross, J. (1977). Towards fatherhood: the epigenesis of paternal identity during a boy's first decade. *International Review of Psychoanalysis*, 4: 327.

Ross, J. (1985/1986). Symposium: The psychology of men: New psychoanalytic perspectives. *Bull. The Assoc. for Psychoanalytic Medicine*, 25.

Ross, J. (1994). *What Men Want: Mothers, Fathers and Manhood. Selected papers of John Munder Ross 1975–1990*. Cambridge, MA: Harvard University Press.

Ross, J. (1999). Once more onto the couch: consciousness and preconscious defenses in the psychoanalytic situation and process. *Journal of the American Psychoanalytic Association*, 47: 1.

Salcedo, H. (1999). El aborto inducido en Colombia: Una exploración local de la experiencia masculina. In: *El Aborto Inducido en Colombia* (pp. 261–313). Cuadernos del CIDS, No. 3, Universidad Externado de Colombia, Bogota.

Sánchez Vázquez, A. (1996). Introducción a la ética. In: G. Careaga, J. Figueroa & M. Mejía (Eds.), *Etica y Salud Reproductiva* (pp. 29–81). Mexico: National Autonomous University of Mexico and Editorial Porrúa.

Sandler, J. (1959). The body as phallus: a patient's fear of erection. *International Journal Psycho-Analysis*, 40: 191–198.

Sayavedra, G., & Flores, M. (1997). *Ser Mujer: ¿un Riesgo Para la Salud?* Mexico: Red de Mujeres, A.C.

Searles, H. (1980). *Escritos Sobre Esquizofrenia*, Ed.Gedisa. Bs.As. 1980 (*Collected Papers of Schizophrenia and Related Subjects*, London: The Hogarth Press, 1966).

Seidler, V. (1989). *Rediscovering Masculinity: Reason, Language, and Sexuality*. New York: Routledge.

Seidler, V. (1997). Masculinidad, discurso y vida emocional. In: J. Figueroa & R. Nava (Eds.), *Memorias del Seminario Taller "Identidad masculina, sexualidad y salud reproductiva"*. Mexico City: El Colegio de México.

Sherfey, M. J. (1966, 1972). *The Nature and Evolution of Female Sexuality*. New York: Random House.

Shweder, R. (1994). What do men want? A Reading List for the Male Identity Crisis. The New York Times Book Review, 9/1/1994.

Simenauer, E. (1954). "Pregnancy envy" in Rainier Maria Rilke. *Amer. Imago II*, 11: 235–248.

Socarides, C. (1968). *The Overt Homosexual*. New York: Grune & Stratton.

Stoller, R. (1968). *Sex and Gender*. London: Karnac, 1984.

Stoller, R. (1975). Healthiest parental influences on the earliest development of masculinity in baby boys. *Psychoanalytic Forum, 5*: 232–262.

Stoller, R., & Herdt, G. (1982). The development of masculinity: a cross-cultural contribution. *Journal of the American Psychoanalytic Association, 30*: 39–59.

Stolorow, R., Atwood, G., & Munder Ross, J. (1978). The representational world in psychoanalytic psychotherapy. International Review of Psycho-analysis, *5*(3): 247–256.

Szasz, I. (1998). Los hombres y la sexualidad: aportes de la perspectiva feminista y primeros acercamientos a su estudio en México. In: S. Lerner (Ed.), *Varones, Sexualidad y Reproducción* (pp. 137–162). Mexico: El Colegio de México.

Tolbert, K., & Morris, K. (1995). Los hombres y la decision de abortar. Latin American Colloquium on Males, Sexuality, and Reproduction, Zacatecas, Mexico (mimeographed).

Tustin, F. (1972). *Autism and Childhood Psychosis*. London: The Hogarth Press Ltd.

Tustin, F. (1981). *Autistic States in Children*. Routledge & Kegan Paul.

Tustin, F. (1990). *The Protective Shell in Children and Adults*. London: Karnac Books.

Tyson, P., & Tyson, R. (1990). Gender development: A theoretical overview. In: *Psychoanalytic Theories of Development*, Chapters 15 and 17. New Haven: Yale University Press.

Tyson, P., & Tyson, R. L. (1990). *Psychoanalytic Theories of Development: An Integration*. New Haven, CT: Yale University Press.

Van Buren, J. (1992). The representation of the maternal body in the symbolic order and the birth of female subjectivity. Paper read in the Argentine Psychoanalytic Association, September 10.

Weber, M. (1947). *The Theory of Economic and Social Organization*. New York: Free Press.

Winnicott, D. W. (1982). Fear of breakdown. *Revista de Psicoanálisis, 4*(2), Buenos Aires.

Wisdom, J. (1983). Male and female. *International Journal of Psycho-Analysis, 64*: 159–168.

Zhou, J.-N., Hofman, M. A., Gooren, L. J. G., & Swaab, D. F. (1995). A sex difference in the human brain and its relation to transsexuality. *Nature, 377*(6552): 68–70.

Zilboorg, (1944). Masculine and feminine. *Psychiatry, 7*: 257–296.